BEXHILL-ON-SEA
A Pictorial History

BEXHILL~ON~SEA
A Pictorial History

Aylwin Guilmant

Phillimore

1982

Published by
PHILLIMORE & CO. LTD.,
London and Chichester

Head Office: Shopwyke Hall,
Chichester, Sussex, England

ISBN 0 85033 453 5

Printed and bound in Great Britain by
BILLING & SONS LIMITED

LIST OF ILLUSTRATIONS

1. Drawing of St. Peter's church before 1878
2. The Bexhill Stone
3. Turner's drawing of martello towers
4. 'Martello Tower' by C. Clarkson Stanfield, R.A.
5. 'The Barracks' by Francis Grose
6. Parish register, 1558
7. Extract from O. S. Map, 1873
8. Town Centre Scheme, 1930
9. Bexhill's first railway station
10. Children on Bexhill beach, early 20th century
11. The 8th Earl De La Warr
12. Mr. John Webb
13. 'A remarkable instance of Longevity'
14. Drawing of St. Peter's church and the De La Warr Pavilion
15. Section of 1867 revision of 1813 O.S. map
16. Downsborough map of Bexhill, 1887
17. Placard showing result of poll, 1894
18. Lt. Col. Henry Lane
19. Charter of Incorporation, 7 April 1902
20. Declaration of war
21. Reading the war news at the Colonnade
22. Local newspaper, 24 September 1887
23. Beating the bounds, 1902
24. 'The Bricks'
25. St Peter's church after restoration of 1878
26. Interior of St. Peter's before restoration
27. As above
28. Interior of St. Peter's after restoration
29. The *Bell* Hotel
30. The Old Town forge, c.1927-8
31. Drawing of exterior of Old Town forge
32. The Manor House, c.1904
33. Detail from window in Manor House
34. High Street, Old Town, c.1890
35. High Street, Old Town, looking east
36. Church Street, Old Town before 1878
37. Church Street from St. Peter's church-yard, 1898
38. Cave Austin's fire-destroyed warehouse, 1908
39. 'Pevensey marshes' by Francis Grose, 1787
40. The old walnut tree, c.1888
41. The old walnut tree, c.1905
42. Belle Hill chapel
43. High Street, Old Town, c.1900
44. Grand Ducal Party, 1897
45. Official programme of Cycling Tournament, 1897
46. Cottages built during Napoleonic Wars
47. Belle Hill, by C. Graves, 1898
48. Belle Hill, by C. Graves, c.1890
49. Herbert Pulham's engineering company
50. Motor bus of Maidstone & District Motor Services
51. Chantry Lane in winter, looking northwards
52. Chantry Lane
53. The Australian cricket team, 1896
54. Mr. Mason of Belmont Dairy, 1915
55. The Down Mill, Sidley
56. Working at the mill
57. Original class at Ancaster House school, 1906
58. Little Common pond in summer
59. Little Common pond frozen
60. Little Common pond in winter
61. Children maypole dancing, Little Common, 1912
62. Cooden Sea Road, Little Common, looking southwards
63. Cooden Sea Road
64. Sackville Road, c.1924
65. Gillham Brothers' workshop
66. Wimshurst's seven cures
67. 'Taking the air' Little Common, c.1910
68. Elliott's grocery and drapery store, Little Common
69. Ninfield Mission Hall Sunday School outing, 1898
70. Unveiling of Little Common War Memorial, 1920
71. Mittens old cottage, c.1900
72. Harriers' meet, Little Common, 1912
73. The *Denbigh* Hotel, 1920
74. Springfield Brass Band, 1911

75. Sidley Infants School, 1918
76. Mr. John Beal with his six sons, 1921
77. John Beal's engineering works, c. 1920
78. Particulars and conditions of sale of Sidley Brickyard and other properties
79. Workers at Adams' Brickworks, Sidley, c. 1900
80. The *Sussex* Inn, Sidley
81. The *Hastings* locomotive, 1902
82. Mrs. Sinden outside her Sidley cottage, 1912
83. John Beal, wheelwright, c. 1910
84. The *New* Inn, Sidley, c. 1890
85. Mr. W. B. Warner outside his hairdressing saloon, Sidley, 1925
86. High Street, Sidley, early 20th century
87. Mrs. Undecimus Stratton, 1904
88. Bexhill Motor Parade, 1902
89. Motor Racing, Whit Monday 1902
90. Egerton Park, c. 1890
91. Playing bowls in Egerton Park
92. Bexhill's second railway station, c. 1891
93. Children watching tennis, Egerton Park
94. The Peace Pageant, 1919
95. Cooden to Hastings trolley buses, 1920
96. Opening of two Secondary schools, 1927
97. De La Warr Parade, c. 1900
98. Plan of the Kursaal
99. Season ticket to the Kursaal, 1901/2
100. Kursaal and ornamental gates of De La Warr Parade
101. Opening of Kursaal by Duches of Teck, 1896
102. The Bexhill Players
103. Eastbourne Aviation Co. flights, 1913
104. Demolition of Sackville Road Cattle Arch, 1892
105. The Cattle Arch, Cooden Drive, c. 1921
106. Bathing machines at Bexhill
107. The Cycle Chalet, 1896
108. The Cycle Track, East Parade
109. Preparation for war, 1939
110. Procession for Lord De La Warr's return from the Boer War, 1900
111. Mr. William Gordon Harris and his sister, 1900
112. Western Road, c. 1900
113. Tea Room on the sea front
114. Sketches of the opening of the New Municipal Building, 1895
115. The Town Hall opening, 1895
116. The Town Hall, 1895
117. Advertisement for electric light, 1899
118. Central Parade, c. 1908
119. West Parade, c. 1908
120. View from Old Town, c. 1870
121. Opening of The Colonnade, 1911
122. Early print of London Road
123. Chalybeate Spring
124. The industrial depression, 1931
125. Gale damage on the sea front, 1912
126. As above
127. As above
128. The village green, Little Common, c. 1910
129. The village green, detail from above
130. Forge Cottage, Little Common
131. Cottage and tea garden, c. 1910
132. Celebration of 25th anniversary of Charter Day, 1927
133. Bexhill Horse Show, 1912
134. Bandstand and Marine Mansions, c. 1900
135. Bexhill Fire Brigade, c. 1912
136. Collington Wood
137. The Maharajah of Cooch Behar, 1913
138. Early beach scene, Bexhill
139. Beach huts, Bexhill
140. Plans of the De La Warr Pavilion
141. Opening of the De La Warr Pavilion, 1935

This book is dedicated

to

all Bexhillians, past and present

PREFACE

This book does not set out to be a history of the town of Bexhill-on-Sea. Rather it is a story of its people as it is they who play an essential part in the making of a town. Bexhill-on-Sea first came into being as a middle-class seaside resort, but times have changed and today's generation prefer to take their holidays abroad. However, the town has become popular as a home for retired people, many of whom came here from far afield and who consequently may know little of the town prior to World War II. I have, therefore, used the war as a cut-off date as many old buildings were demolished in the name of progress during the 1950s and 1960s. Those that remain stand as sentinels of the past. In illustrating the character and growth of the town before 1939, I am also portraying a way of life that, perhaps sadly, is no longer with us.

ACKNOWLEDGEMENTS

My sincere thanks go to the Editor, John Cornelius, and the Deputy Editor, John Dowling of *The Bexhill-on-Sea Observer* for permission to research their archives and the free use of many of their photographs. I am also indebted to The Bexhill Museum Association and particularly to the Curator, Mr. H. Sargent, for the loan of many of their photographs and the use of the material therein. I must also thank Mrs. Pamela Haines, the Bexhill Area Librarian and members of the staff of the Bexhill Library for the help given me in researching this book, Hastings Museum and in particular Ms. Victoria Williams, and Hastings Library, Rother District Council, Earl De La Warr, the Rector of Bexhill, the Reverend Michael Townroe and members of the Old Town Preservation Association.

I wish to record my debt to Mrs. Bartley and F. J. Parsons (Westminster Press Ltd.) for the free use of *The Story of Bexhill* by the late L. J. Bartley; I have referred to this book as a source for many of the captions to the photographs and without reference to this volume, much of my book would not have been possible. In this connection, also, I would like to thank Dr. V. Hanley for correcting the original text.

The photographic work for the book was carried out by Mr. Robert Cook. As a work of this sort is entirely dependent upon the photographer's skill, I am grateful in the extreme for all that Robert has done for me. Where I have used photographs not yet out of copyright, I have acknowledged them individually, but there may be a few instances where copyright may have been infringed. If there are such copyright owners whose works have inadvertently been reproduced without permission, I hope that they will accept my apologies. In this connection I must thank the Victoria and Albert Museum, the Portal Gallery and the *Observer* magazine.

The author is greatly indebted to the kind and willing co-operation of the many people, too numerous to mention individually, who have so generously lent pictures from their family albums, without which this book would not have been possible. I apologise for any inaccuracies that may have arisen. It is very difficult in a work such as this to identify everyone in a particular photograph, but I have tried to be as precise as possible.

BIBLIOGRAPHY

Anderson, J., & Swinglehurst, E., *The Victorian and Edwardian Seaside,* 1978.

Brabant, F. G., & Jessup, Ronald F., *The Little Guides, Sussex,* 9th Ed., 1938.

Bartley, L. J., *The Story of Bexhill,* (Bexhill-on-Sea) 1971.

Cannadine, David, *Lords and Landlords the Aristocracy and the Towns 1774-1967,*(Leicester University Press) 1980.

Diplock, W., *The Hastings Guide.*

Earwaker, Clifford, *The Story of St. Peter's Bexhill,* (Bexhill-on-Sea) 1938.

Hern, Anthony, *The Seaside Holiday,* 1967.

Horsfield, T. W., *The History, Antiquities and Topography of the County of Sussex,*1835.

Kelly's Directories of Sussex.

Mullens, W. H.,*A short History of Bexhill in the County of Sussex,* (Bexhill-on-Sea) 1927.

Pilkington, M. C., *Bexhill a study in the growth of a seaside town,* (1952) Unpublished thesis.

Sussex Archaeological Collections, vol. 53.

The Sussex County Magazine.

Seaside Watering Places Season 1896-97. Published by Gill L. Upcott, no author given.

Ward Lock & Co.'s *Illustrated Guide Books Series 1897-98, 1922-23 and 1934-35.*

Wood, Neville, *Health Resorts of the British Islands,* 1912.

Victoria County History of Sussex.

All Saints' Church, Sidley.

The Bexhill Town Guide.

Bexhill Old Town Guide.

Bexhill-on-Sea Illustrated, (no author given) 1901.

Bygone Bexhill (a pamphlet issued by the Bexhill Museum. No author given).

Bexhill Grammar School Golden Jubilee 1926-1976.

Files of the *Bexhill-on-Sea Observer* and the *Bexhill Chronicle.*

INTRODUCTION AND BRIEF HISTORY OF BEXHILL-ON-SEA

The word Bexhill is a most unfortunate corruption of Bexle, the ancient name of the place. It first occurs in its modern form towards the end of the 15th century (*Sussex Archaeological Collections*, vol. 53, p. 61). An early spelling of the name gives Bexlea, later becoming Bexelei in Domesday Book, and having several variations in the following years.

The official guide book for 1904 states that Bexhill consisted of an ancient village upon a hill (overlooking Pevensey Bay), the sea a half mile distant. The place possesses a history from A.D. 772. The 'Catularum Saxonicum' records that Offa, granted Bishop Oswald a grant of land for life at Bexlei with reversion to the See. On this land was built the parish church of St. Peter's over 1200 years ago, the oldest part being hidden in the walls. The original charter is not extant, but a medieval document in the Lambeth records, written in Latin, defines the bounds of the church lands in Anglo-Saxon. While this medieval document is regarded as a copy of the original, it is no doubt based on a genuine grant and the boundaries may be accepted as at least pre-Conquest (L. J. Bartley, *The Story of Bexhill*, 1971, p. 5).

One of the town's most precious and interesting objects, an 8th-century carved stone, was found during the restoration of St. Peter's church in 1878.

Following the Battle of Hastings in 1066, Bexhill was devastated, and the Domesday survey made 20 years later showed that it had not recovered its original worth. Duke William of Normandy rewarded his principal captains with gifts of land, and to his cousin Robert, 2nd Count of Eu he gave the Rape of Hastings, which included Bexhill then comprising 60 hides.

Apart from the Manor of Bexhill, owned successively by the Church, the Rape of Hastings, again owned by the Church, and, after an interval in the hands of the Crown, by the Sackville family, there were several other manors on the outskirts of the area, covered by the present borough (*The Story of Bexhill*, p. 6), among them being Barnhorne, Buckholt, Cooden, Glyne, Gotham, Northeye, Pebsham (a name subject to various spellings over the ages) and Worsham; all names in existence today.

The Batesford Chantry within the church was built in the middle of the 15th century, and it is clear that the endowment was derived from the Chantry Farm, now known as Church Farm, and today the rectory of St. Peter's church. During the reign of Elizabeth I this chapel was used as a schoolroom (Clifford Earwaker, *The Story of St. Peter's, Bexhill*, 1959, p. 15); thus came into being the first school at Bexhill.

The Saxon village of Bexhill is today known as the 'Old Town'. During the 16th century the Manor of Bexhill was given to the Sackville family (their

1. St. Peter's church before the restoration of 1878. In the 18th century, the ugly galleries on three sides of the church, with their dormer windows and high pews, were introduced as a temporary feature to increase the seating, but they remained in use for over one hundred years. At the time of their demolition, the south aisle was enlarged and the chancel extended. Certain interesting features were revealed when wall plaster was removed, including a small painted figure of an evangelist and an interesting fresco; unfortunately, neither of these paintings could be preserved. Also found were two lines of irregular rubble and ashlar work marking the junction of the north and east walls in the old Saxon church. A Celtic stone of the 8th century and a large monumental slab of sandstone with a floreated cross were discovered under the surface in the north aisle, said to be from the tomb of a Crusader. A stone of somewhat similar character marks the resting place of Stephen Langton in Canterbury Cathedral. These two slabs have now been mounted in the tower on the south and north walls respectively.

2. The Bexhill Stone is the earliest
relic of the town and is to be found
mounted in a case on the south side
of St. Peter's tower. It is a remark-
ably fresh 8th century carved stone
which was discovered in 1878 about
six inches under the nave floor near
the first Norman pier on the south
side. Reverend L. S. Clarke, the then
Rector, was inclined to think that
this formed the lid of a child's stone
coffin, but all the evidence is against
this. The elaborate interlaced cable
ornament cut into the stone, familiar in Saxon work and showing
Celtic influence, could never have
been intended for burial out of
sight. Most modern archaeologists
agree that this splendid piece of
work was done by a craftsman from
the north, almost certainly about
the time of St. Wilfrid, and probably
was the lid of a reliquary (containing
the relics of saints) which was placed
within the original church at the
time of its consecration. This
Bexhill Stone, as it is called, has
aroused very great interest among
students all over the country. The
freshness and beauty of the craftsman-
ship have remained through nearly
twelve centuries and it is hard to
realise that it has so long a history.

name is perpetuated today in a street and hotel of that name). For 200 years little of importance occurred until 1729 when a freak storm caused much local devastation which became the subject of a London pamphlet. In 1748 the *Amsterdam* (a Dutch East-Indiaman carrying valuable cargo, much of which was saved) was wrecked off-shore and even into the next century the poor of Bexhill were still digging in the sand-covered hull at Bulverhythe.

The routine of local life, dominated by the Church, the manor, the parish vestry and the agricultural year was more permanently upset by the French Revolution and the Napoleonic wars, which saw the building of 12 martello towers along the foreshore, as well as the building of an infantry depot of the King's German Legion and the laying out of the Parade Ground (*The Story of Bexhill*, p. 28). It is difficult to envisage the tremendous impact the garrisoning of 5,000 troops must have had on a hamlet of 500 persons.

3. This picture has often been misinterpreted as, originally, it was thought to be a view of some of the martello towers at Bexhill. It was painted by J. M. W. Turner and published in his *Liber Studorum* in 1817. The towers seen begin with No. 39 on the site of the present St. Leonard's bathing pool and extend to Galley Hill, Bexhill. Typical of Turner's artistic licence, Bexhill is faintly seen high up beyond the cliffs of Marina, St. Leonards, on the right. Bexhill was then, of course, a small village inland and on a hill top. The water in the lower right foreground is the Bulrush Pond, over which the *Royal Victoria* Hotel was built in 1829.

4. Martello tower between Bexhill and St. Leonards. Engraving after a painting by C. Clarkson Stanfield, R.A.

5. The only known picture in existence showing *The Barracks* at Bexhill, painted by Francis Grose in 1787. This well known antiquary and draughtsman travelled through Sussex painting scenes from life. He was particularly interested in military buildings having been adjutant and paymaster in the Hampshire Militia. The parade ground is thought to have been on land north of Belle Hill, but the actual site of the Barracks has not been located. However, there is some supposition that this may have been on land south of Belle Hill where 'Millfield' now stands.

Francis Grose's other paintings in this collection relating to Bexhill show St. Peter's church, the Manor House and its farm buildings; an unidentified house, the *Wheatsheaf* Inn at Little Common and various lanes leading to the Old Town.

In the past such industry as existed in Bexhill was almost completely devoted to local needs and, in particular, to those of the farming community. There were forges to cater for these needs; one each in Little Common and the Old Town, and in several other areas within the town boundaries, and two in Sidley.

During 1804, when wells were being dug for the King's German Legion, thin bands of lignite, formed from driftwood, were found and mistakenly identified as coal. (Today this is still visible in much of the rock strata.) A company was formed to mine this and some £80,000 was reported to have been spent in unsuccessful borings at the bottom of the Down and near the present Ashdown Road, where the workings, including surface buildings, were obliterated when the railway was built.

6. The first page of the Parish Register of St. Peter's church dated 30 November 1558. The earliest register is a transcript made by the then Rector, Dr. Pye, from original manuscript papers kept by him. At the beginning of the book he writes 'This Register was faithfully compiled of the scattering papers beforetime used according to the constitution Provinciall, Doctor of Diuninitie, the Originalles being accordingly delivered into the Commissaries Office at Lewes. In which years the said T. Pye repayred the chauntry chappel on the north side of the chauncel & turned it into a Schole-house'. The first entry records the death of William Williams of Bulverhide (Bulverhythe).

The registers of St. Peter's Church (at present housed in the East Sussex Record Office) commencing in 1558, record the weddings of officers, N.C.O.s and men to Bexhill brides, a number of whom went to Hanover to set up home after the long war ended.

7. Extracts reproduced from part of the Ordnance Survey of Bexhill dated 1873 (scale 1:2500). St. Peter's church is clearly defined; the Manor House (at this time called 'Court Lodge') is also shown. Cheeseman's Farm was sited on land that later in the century became the site of the Metropolitan Convalescent Institution and today is known as East Down House. Chantry Farm is today known as Church Farm and is the rectory. Barrack Hall, originally the officers quarters during the garrisoning of the town by the King's German Legion, is now a refuge for battered wives, known as St. Jude's.

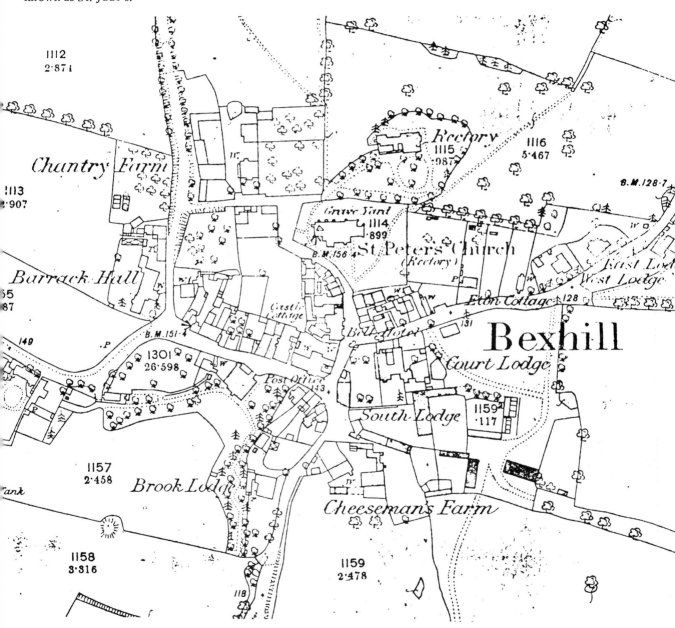

At the beginning of the 18th century Bexhill was a small village consisting of a few houses clustered around the church of St. Peter, the Manor House and the village inn (now the *Bell* Hotel). A narrow lane, today Sea Road, led from this settlement on the hill through cornfields to the marshy land and sea shore. Much of the countryside to the south of the village was uncultivated, low-lying and transversed by ditches; at times it was inundated by the sea.

The Ordnance Survey Map of 1813 showed the many windmills which covered the Bexhill skyline, especially on the high ground to the north. Today only the brick roundels of the Down Mill and of Pankhurst Mill at Sidley remain as evidence, where there had been at least three mills. Also recorded is a mill at Barnhorn, but this had vanished before 1813.

The revised 1873 Ordnance Survey map marks the start of the expansion towards the town we know today. At that time Bexhill population was just over 2,000 and there were some four hundred and fifty houses (both figures estimated ones). Today the 1981 census shows the population to be 36,000, with 16,345 dwellings.

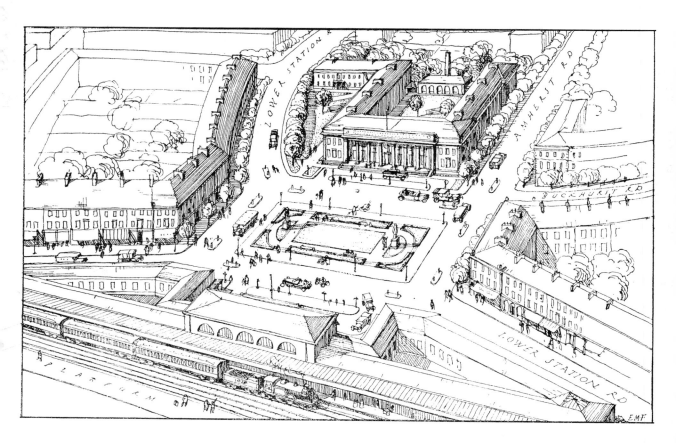

8. The Town Centre Scheme was advocated by the planning consultants Adams Thompson and Fry of Westminster, in a report to the Corporation on the development of Bexhill in 1930. It envisaged a new railway station fronting Town Hall Square, and also a loop line connecting the south coast route with the then Bexhill West to Crowhurst branch line.

Poor communications with other parts of the country made the village of Bexhill largely dependent on its own resources. Brickmaking became important, and there were a number of small yards at various places, the locations later being changed as the clay was 'worked out' (*The Story of Bexhill*, p. 93). One of the last of these small yards to operate was that of the Adams family at Sidley.

The most important factor in the rise of modern Bexhill-on-Sea was the coming of the railway in 1846, when the London Brighton and South Coast Company opened its single line between Lewes and Bulverhythe. It ran wholly through fields in the parish, for Bexhill was still the village on the hill; however, much of the land in the area belonged to the De La Warr Estate and the then Earl stipulated that Bexhill should have a railway halt, and so this station was built on the north side of the line; with the growth of Bexhill-on-Sea south of the railway, a new station fronting Devonshire Square was built in 1891, but early in the next century this was moved to its present site at Sea Road.

9. Bexhill's first station on the Lewes-Bulverhythe railway opened in 1846 on the north side of the line. With the growth of Bexhill south of the railway, a new station fronting Devonshire Square was built in 1891 and the accommodation on the north side was improved. Cattle pens at one time abutted the old station.

Bexhill was the first of the seaside resorts to allow 'mixed' bathing, and as early as 1896 guide books described 'the bathing is a great feature of the town, and level sands can be enjoyed by young and old with perfect safety' (*Seaside Watering Places*, 1896-7 season, p. 136).

As early as 1813 the *Star* newspaper had advertised property for sale in Bexhill and stated that it is 'one of the most healthy and pleasant situations on the Coast of Sussex, and well adapted for sea-bathing, for which purpose it is occasionally resorted to!'

Beside the sea bathing facilities already mentioned, there were available various forms of medical baths in the town, including vapour, hot air, iodine, tannic acid and electrical baths; according to the advertisement these all took place at The Hydro (*Health Resorts of the British Islands*, p. 168).

10. Children enjoying the pleasures of the beach early this century. In the background are houses on the De La Warr Parade, looking very similar today. South and west of these houses on the beach, was built the Kursaal and later this century, the Bexhill Sailing Club.

Many of the seaside resorts grew through the influence of aristocratic involvement, as they were dependent on land-owners' finance and enterprise, and so tended to offer considerable scope for the wielding of aristocratic power in an urban context (David Cannadine, *Lords and Landlords the Aristocracy in the Towns, 1774-1967*, 1980, p. 63). Bexhill was no exception and while it unmistakably bore this aristocratic stamp it was built to serve predominantly a middle-class type of visitor. Neville Wood, in his book *Health Resorts of the British Islands*, 1912, p. 168, describes it thus:

> The population is annually recruited by many Anglo-Indians, and visitors from the Continent are numerous particularly from France. As has been already indicated the 'tripper' element is not encouraged, nor is it in evidence at Bexhill at any time of year . . . while the beach minstrel and pierrot type of entertainment is escaped at Bexhill, this resort has attained a reputation for music provided at various places of entertainment . . .

To the east of the 'old town' lay the fishing village of Hastings and later in the 19th century the resort of St. Leonards. Diplock's *Guide to Hastings* published in the mid-century mentioned Bexhill 'about six miles to the west' as a 'most delightful ride along the coast' and added:

> There is a good and convenient inn with every accommodation calculated for the reception of strangers, who in Summer, are frequently induced to visit this rural spot. Very recently a few lodging houses, a circulating library and a small theatre have been erected . . .

The inn was, of course, the *Bell*. The theatre became its assembly room (*The Story of Bexhill* and *The Hastings Guide 1820*). Among early visitors to Bexhill were Princess Victoria (later Queen) and her mother, who paid a visit to the 'village' while staying in St. Leonards, and in 1864 her son, Edward, Prince of Wales (the future King Edward VII).

To the west of the hamlet was the village of Little Common, originally called Slyder's Common, and to the north, Sidley, where the local smugglers fought their last battle with the Preventive force on Sidley Green in 1828. Both these villages were surrounded by farms which they served.

It was in the 1880s that the De La Warrs, a family of Kentish landowners, began to create Bexhill. Like many landowners at this time the slump in agriculture led them to plough their money into the development of seaside resorts. The De La Warrs rationalized their holdings of land in other areas in order to expand locally; however, many of their projects failed through lack of sufficient finance. In 1883, the 7th Earl constructed the sea wall, and thereafter laid out parades and promoted the local gas and water companies. It was he who added the words 'On-Sea' to its name in 1884, thereby announcing its intention of joining the seaside resort race. *The Complete Peerage* gives a figure of the Earl's holdings in Sussex for the year 1883 as 17,185 acres. His son, the future 8th Earl, lived in the manor house at Bexhill from 1891 and in 1894 his father made over to him with a life interest the management of the family's estates in the town which were entailed and subject to the control of trustees. Viscount Cantelupe married a daughter of the 1st Baron (afterwards Earl) Brassey of Normanhurst and set the pattern for Bexhill's golden decade of the 1890s. Almost the whole of the town's development as a high-class, late-Victorian and Edwardian seaside resort was due to him (*The Hastings Guide*, p. 19 and *The Story of Bexhill*). The family built The Kursaal as a centre for local entertainment, and financed the construction of the *Sackville*, a high-class hotel in the grand manner. The 8th Earl turned the manor house into a 'Mecca' for his aristocratic friends.

> He himself was a chairman of the Urban Council and the Incorporation Committee, and was unashamedly the most powerful local resident. But his departure for the Boer War and the town's incorporation in 1902 witnessed a major shift in the balance of power, as initiative and influence passed into the hands of local leadership. Yet for another generation and more, the De La Warrs and the Earls Brassey, their near neighbours and relatives, enjoyed an Indian summer of prestige and social leadership, as each family provided, in successive generations, mayors of the borough. When the 8th Earl died on active service in 1915, he was mourned as 'the maker of modern Bexhill (*Lords and Landlords*, p. 66).

A glittering event of this decade was the opening of the Town Hall which took place in April 1895 and it was the Earl who was responsible for inviting the Lord Mayor of London, Sir Joseph Renals, to perform the opening ceremony.

In 1902, the year which saw the end of the South African war and the coronation of King Edward VII, Bexhill received its Charter of Incorporation. At this time the town was still expanding; parade walls had been constructed and the laying out of thoroughfares and erection of private dwellings, shops and hotels continued. By the early years of the present century the professional, commercial and shopping centre of the town was almost exclusively south of the railway. The Bexhill-Crowhurst branch line (axed in 1964) was opened with fast trains to Charing Cross. A new police station was built, the Clock Tower on the West Parade was erected, the laying out of Egerton Park was well advanced, and proposals for the construction of a pier were under consideration. In this memorable year, too, 'Bexhill was given over to the horseless vehicles which monopolised the streets making the place hum with rattling machinery and causing a cyclonic disturbance of the air as they flew past' (*Bygone Bexhill*, unpublished pamphlet, Bexhill Museum). This was the first motor-car 'meet' in Britain and took place along the De La Warr Parade. At that time the population was 13,000 and the rates 1s. 10d. in the pound.

In 1909 the Corporation began the Central Parade, virtually linking the eastern and western sections, and with this were laid out gardens including the 'religious lawn'. The Central Parade was opened in 1910 and was followed by the building of the Colonnade. Bexhill's most famous building, the De La Warr Pavilion, lies to the north of the Colonnade on land which was originally known as 'the Horn' and on which stood martello tower No. 47 and, later in the last century, the Coastguard Station. In rough weather the sea would virtually isolate 'the Horn', sweeping up Sackville Road as far as the Arch (then a cattle access) and along Sea Road to where St. Barnabas Church now stands. The Urban Council obtained control of an open space, now known as Bexhill Down, but formerly called Bexhill Common. The laying out of the Down with the 'ridings', which remain today, was one of the first works of the Council's Surveyor of that time, Mr. George Ball. In 1901 the Urban Council leased and then bought Egerton Park from Mr. John Webb, and at once proceeded to landscape the grounds in their present form. In 1903, a shelter hall, now the Museum, was built in the park as a concert hall (*The Story of Bexhill*, p. 134).

11. Gilbert George Reginald Viscount Cantelupe (1869-1915), who, at the age of 26, succeeded as 8th Earl De La Warr following the death of his father in January 1896. Among many aspects of all that he did for Bexhill, an important place should be given to his local government work. He was first elected to the local Board of Health in 1892, and two years later to the town's first Urban Council of which he became Chairman after the death of Colonel Henry Lane in 1895. Viscount Cantelupe married in 1891 Muriel (second daughter of the 1st Baron, afterwards Earl) Brassey of Normanhurst. His heir, and only son, Herbert Brassey Sackville, was born in 1900. This marriage was terminated in divorce two years later and he was the victim of a campaign of some viciousness. Due to this event, the Earl was overlooked as a candidate for the mayoralty of the Borough. However, the next year the Town Council made amends by inviting Earl De La Warr to become Mayor, and he held the office for two years during which he became an Alderman. Earl De La Warr married for the second time in 1903, Miss Hilda Clavering, who survived him. He built the Kursaal as a place of entertainment, and his social leadership and influence in bringing notable visitors to the town promoted its growth. The Earl inspired the first motor races in England and it is, of course, entirely due to him that Bexhill has the famous Cooden Golf Club, whose course was opened in 1912. Indeed, his vast expenditure on promoting Bexhill eventually led him into financial difficulties and he was twice involved in bankruptcy proceedings. During the Boer War, the Earl had been a war correspondent for the *Globe*, and at the outbreak of the 1914 war he volunteered for active service and was eventually given a temporary commission in the Royal Navy. Taken ill on returning to the Dardanelles campaign, he died aged 46, in the presence of his mother and sister, at Messina, Sicily, in December 1915. The Italian authorities paid a notable tribute of respect, and both civil and military dignitaries attended the funeral which was accompanied by full military honours. In Bexhill the news was received with genuine sorrow as he was remembered for his immense service to the town of which he was the leading and most colourful character in the history of its development.

Mr. Webb, with great foresight, had accepted land (in part payment for his construction of the eastern sea wall undertaken on behalf of the Earl De La Warr) south of the railway and west of Sea Road, which he developed energetically, including what is known today as West Parade.

12. Mr. John Webb, a south London builder and contractor, first became involved in the growth of the seaside resort of Bexhill-on-Sea, when he surveyed and undertook to build a sea wall and esplanade between Galley Hill and Sea Lane (now Road), embanking the marshy ground behind. The contract for this work was £34,000 and work was completed in 1883. Three years later, as part of his development of the Egerton Park Estate, Mr. Webb entered into an agreement with the 7th Earl to build a western promenade and adjoining roads which stood out like causeways above the marshy ground that is now Egerton Park and the Polegrove. In part payment for work on the East and De La Warr Parades, Mr. Webb accepted land south of the railway and west of Sea Lane, which he developed with much courage in difficult years, as trade and residential properties. Mr. Webb laid out Western Road and built the *Devonshire* Hotel becoming the first licensee. He laid out the first part of Egerton Park which was later taken over by the then Urban Council at the turn of the century. Mr. Webb constructed the park lake by the drainage and diversion of rivulets and during this work an Iguanadon vertebra and an ancient boat were found. In 1888 Mr. Webb laid out the first tennis courts and the next year made a primitive swimming bath, lining an old salting depression with concrete and bringing sea water through an iron pipe. Mr. Webb had been involved with promoting a Parliamentary Bill to provide water and gas supplies in the growing town. However, the Earl and a number of residents succeeded in getting Mr. Webb's Bill rejected by a House of Lords Select Committee. The next year Lord De La Warr himself, with several Hastings businessmen who had begun to speculate in residential building in Bexhill, formed the Bexhill Water and Gas Company and promoted a Bill which was unopposed and received Parliamentary sanction in June 1885. Mr. Webb died in 1922, an octogenarian, having been responsible for much of the town centre as it stands today.

Four acres of waste ground adjoining the Park were turned into a park extension which was opened in the Summer of 1906 by the Lord Mayor of London. It was in this extension that the Corporation built the 'Pergola', a popular entertainment rendezvous. The 13 acres of land known as the 'Pole Grove' were purchased also from Mr. Webb in 1912, levelled by municipal tippings, and formally opened as a recreation ground in 1923 (now the well-known venue of 'The Bexhill Horse Show' held for many years on Whit Monday) and called today 'the Polegrove'.

Another contributory factor in the rise of Bexhill was the number of independent schools which opened within the boundaries of the town. Before the 1939 war Bexhill could boast over fifty; after this war the number had dwindled to 14, today the figure is three. After Thomas Pye's use of the Chantry chapel as a 'schole' house during his rectorship of St. Peter's between 1589 and 1609, there is no record of continuity in education until the middle of the 19th century, when there is mention only of one John Dann who was appointed school-master in 1775. There is on record, however, a school known as the 'Wilson Memorial School' being housed in three wooden cottages built by the King's German Legion; these cottages were finally demolished in 1962 (*The Story of Bexhill*, p. 85).

Bexhill was increasingly favoured as a place of retirement, especially by those with Indian and Far East associations, and had been a place where they sent their sons and daughters to be educated, while they remained abroad. One of the town's best-known inhabitants was Lt.-Col. Henry Lane (a veteran of the Indian Mutiny) who became 'the father of local government' in Bexhill. A memorial to commemorate his achievements was erected in Town Hall Square in the last century.

When the town began to expand, both as a residential and holiday resort, there was an influx of tradesmen, chiefly from the Sussex countryside, to meet the new demands, and many of their daughters found employment in domestic service. Directories of the period show trades which have now vanished; there were basket-makers, bath chairmen, carriers, fly proprietors, livery stables, oil and colourmen, luggage porters, wheelwrights and window-blind makers (*The Story of Bexhill*, p. 94 and *Kelly's Directories of Sussex*). The *Sackville* Hotel had its own Mews and there were others in Sackville Road and in Station Road.

Mention has already been made of the two railway stations in the town proper, that of the Central and Bexhill West. Rival schemes for the promotion of a tramway service at Bexhill dated from 1897, and culminated in the formation of the Hastings and District Electric Tramway Company Limited in 1904. The laying of Bexhill's tramlines began in Endwell Road in May of the following year, and Sea Road Bridge was widened to accommodate the new traffic. In July 1906 the tram service was extended to Cooden, the greater part of this section running through open fields. In 1907 the Town Council rejected a move to ask the company to extend the service to Sidley. However, from 1901 the Urban Council had granted licences to the Bexhill Motor Company of Sackville Road who ran a fleet of four 14-seater Daimler omnibuses between Hastings, Sidley, Ninfield and Little Common (*The Story of Bexhill*, p. 154).

During nearly 150 years Bexhill has been honoured with more royal visits than might have been expected for a town of its size. The Duchess of Teck (mother of Queen Mary) opened the Kursaal at Whitsun 1896. Two of Queen Victoria's grand-daughters are remembered for opening a Church Army Home in 1907 and the Bexhill Hospital in May 1933. October 1930 saw the first of two visits by the Duke of York (afterwards King George VI) who first came as president of the Queen's Hospital for Children to open an annexe to the Little Folk's Home at Little Common. His second visit, when he was accompanied by the Duchess (now the Queen Mother), was in December 1935 to open the De La Warr Pavilion.

A Remarkable instance of Longevity.

THE undermentioned 46 persons, Inhabitants of the Parish of BEXHILL, assembled together at the Bell Inn, on the 4th of June, 1819, to commemorate the *Eighty-first* Anniversary of the birth of our beloved Sovereign King George the Third, whose ages, taken on an average, were as follows :—Twenty-five, who dined, 81 years—Fifteen, who waited at Table, 71 years, and Six, who rung a merry peal on the Church Bells whilst the above were at Dinner, 61 years, leaving a surplus of 2 years and 7 months. They were selected from the whole Male Population, which does not exceed a thousand.

THE DINNER PARTY.

Names.	Ages. Yr.	Mo.	Names.	Ages. Yr.	Mo.	Names.	Ages. Yr.	Mo.
William Duke ... *President*	83	11	John Page	82	6	John Easton	78	6
John Hammond.. *Vice-president*	82	4	William Prior	82	6	Wakeham Coleman	78	6
Thomas Longhurst	87	9	Joseph Godwin	82	3	Thomas Reeves	77	9
John Vidler	87	6	Thomas Curtiss	82	0	William Wellfare	77	9
Nicholas Mewett	86	5	Henry Clifton	81	6	Ever. Cruttenden	77	8
Peter Elliott	83	11	Henry Freeman	80	9	John Gilham	77	4
John Godwin	83	10	Jacob Young	80	5	John Cramp	77	0
			Thomas Eastwood	80	0	William Miller	76	3
			William Mewett	79	8	William Weeks	75	3

WAITERS.

Names.	Ages. Yr.	Mo.	Names.	Ages. Yr.	Mo.	Names.	Ages. Yr.	Mo.
John Tap	74	7	Thomas Munn	73	1	John Maplesden	69	7
John Leonard	74	0	Joseph Carey	73	0	Thomas Sands	69	7
William Chatfield	73	8	Samuel Easton	72	8	William Edmonds	69	6
John Duke	73	8	John Christian	72	6	William Winborn	69	3
William Dunk	73	3	William Mitten	70	0	Edward Spray	68	9

RINGERS.

Names.	Ages. Yr.	Mo.	Names.	Ages. Yr.	Mo.	Names.	Ages. Yr.	Mo.
John Lansdell	65	9	Thomas Roberts	62	9	Samuel Burgess	60	0
William Lansdell	62	8	Samuel Sinden	61	8	Richard Fairway	56	2

Bayley, Letter-press and Copper-plate Printer, Bookbinder, Stationer, &c. Battle

13. Old age in Bexhill has for many years been more than a jest. On King George III's birthday, a dinner for aged residents was held at the *Bell* Hotel. This poster relates the occasion.

Bexhill has long been renowned for its 'healthy air'; as early as 1881 the Metropolitan Convalescent Institution was built on the southern slopes of the

Old Town. In 1905 the Institution built the home at Cooden and this became the men's home, the one in the Old Town being reserved for women patients. Nazareth Home in Hastings Road, built in 1894 as a permanent home for aged and infirm of both sexes, also for incurable and orphaned girls, was and is run by the Sisters of Nazareth, a branch of the Hammersmith home of the same name.

In conclusion, Bexhill as a health resort has long been noted for the longevity of its inhabitants; indeed it has been a standing joke that a person may live here as long as he chooses! A story is told in this connection of a banquet held at the *Bell* Inn in the 'old village' in the year 1819, when the male population was considerably under one thousand. Twenty-five venerable patriarchs, all over eighty-one, sat down to the feast, being waited upon by 15 others all over seventy-one, while six 'youths' of 61 and upwards enlivened the proceedings by playing a peal on the bells of the church across the way (Ward Lock & Co., *Illustrated Guide Books series*, 1922-23).

There can be little doubt that the extreme healthiness of Bexhill is due to the purity and invigorating character of the air. Ward Lock guidebooks throughout this century have described the climate as ' . . . bracing and equable. The open situation of the town renders the air much keener than at neighbouring resorts'.

Bexhill today is a vastly different place to the town that grew into being 100 years ago. No longer may it be described as 'une petite ville coquette' from the fact that the town had not a little suggestion of the Continental resort about it; a lightness and gaiety that are, however, duly and discreetly modified to the requirements of British taste (*Health Resorts of the British Islands*, p. 166).

In 1884 the parish became Bexhill-on-Sea, and was governed by a Local Board. Its growth was rapid and in 1894 this was superseded by an Urban District Council. On 7 April 1902 it was granted a Charter incorporating it as a Municipal Borough (M. C. Pilkington, *Bexhill, A Study in a Growth of a Seaside Town*. Unpublished thesis, p. 16).

Seventy-two years of civic independence for Bexhill ceased to exist and Rother district came into being. The 1972 Local Government Act which created the new district authorities was so framed that Bexhill as a town was either too big or too small for its provisions. As a result it could neither continue its independence as did Hastings, nor retain some of the trappings as did Rye. Consquently, Bexhill, with its many scattered villages merged with the ancient towns of Battle and Rye. When Bexhill was first granted a Charter of incorporation the borough was divided into five wards and the first municipal elections were held in that year.

The first mayor to be appointed was Mr. Ebenezer Howard (who had inherited the Birchington estate but had never taken part in public life). After Mr. Howard's initial year, Earl De La Warr was mayor for two years, and he, with his son the 9th Earl, who was mayor from 1932-35, provide with the 1st Earl Brassey and his son, the 2nd and last Earl, the only instances of father and son occupying the civic chair. The Howard, De La Warr and Brassey mayoralties with the first of Daniel Mayer's four years in 1905-06 were notable in that the holders were not members of the Council at the time of their election as mayor (*The Story of Bexhill*, p. 47). The final mayor in this sequence of events was Councillor Harold Morgan. So came to an end the 10th and last borough to be created in Sussex after nearly seventy-two years of civic independence.

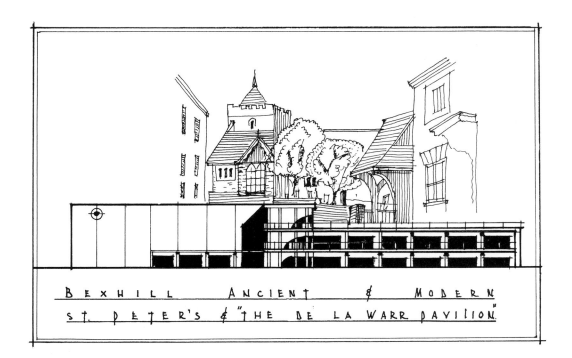

BEXHILL ANCIENT & MODERN
ST. PETER'S & "THE DE LA WARR PAVILION"

OLD TOWN

The Bexhill Old Town, a typical Sussex trilogy, consisted of the Church, the Manor and the Farm; today St. Peter's church still stands, the manor has been demolished and the farm house has become the rectory. A highly-respected medical practitioner, Dr. Wills, for many years an inhabitant of the Old Town, wrote in the 1870s that it 'must have been a most picturesque spot, a tiny village crowded in between the venerable church and ancient manor house nestling among trees and looking down across breezy slopes onto the white coastguard station and the open channel'. An Ordnance Survey map of Bexhill for the middle of the 19th century shows that Bexhill then was virtually only this settlement in the Old Town. The area to the south consisted entirely of farm land, the aforementioned coastguard cottages on 'the Horn' and an occasional farm house. Diplock's *Guide of Hastings* of the mid century mentions that 'a few lodging houses, a circulating library and a small theatre have been erected and Mr. Brook, a respectable resident, keeps a most excellent pack of hounds which in the winter and sporting seasons affords recreation and amusement'. The inn was, of course, the *Bell*, the theatre became its assembly room, and Mr. John Brook resided at the Manor House, then known as Court Lodge (L. J. Bartley, *The Story of Bexhill*, 1971, p. 29).

The first church in Bexhill would have been in the simple Saxon style of nave and square-ended sanctuary, with walls of irregular rubble and ashlar. When William and his forces marched inland to do battle with Harold they would have seen this little Saxon Church of St. Peter. It may well have been some of his capable and experienced stone masons from Normandy who, having built Battle Abbey, came here to replace a small building with a larger and stronger Norman edifice. Its massive tower could have served as a look-out post across the marshes to Pevensey and out to sea (*Bexhill Old Town Preservation Society Booklet*). Early in the 13th century the small Norman sanctuary was replaced by a noble Early English one. About 1450 a south chapel was added and at the same time the Chantry Chapel on the north side was built. The growth of population led to the introduction of ugly galleries in the 18th century, and these were removed in 1878 when the south aisle was enlarged and the chancel extended. Again in 1906 the accommodation was further extended by the building of a new north aisle.

A small military camp had been based at Bexhill since the 18th century and the men had been involved in building some of the martello towers along the coastline, but in 1804 several thousand men from the King's German Legion were billeted in barracks which were built on some 25 acres of land which lay on the north of Belle Hill from the Old Town. Major-General Sir Arthur

Wellesley, later the Duke of Wellington, who was for a time stationed at Hastings, is reputed to have stayed at Barrack Hall, which was then the Officers' Mess.

In 1819, on George III's 81st birthday, a party was given at the *Bell* for 46 people all over 75, the oldest being eighty-seven. Of those who attended this event only three died under 80 and several lived to be over 92, which was a record in those days. Their long lives had been thought to be due to the healthy, bracing climate of the town.

There was no industry within the Old Town but nevertheless it was a self-supporting community; a forge to cater for the local agricultural needs stood at the top of what is now Upper Sea Road. This was demolished after the Second World War. The Pocock family opened their first butcher's shop and slaughter house in about 1770 and in 1801 moved into their present premises.

The Manor House, originally a fortified Bishop's Palace, was the main building in the Old Town, with the exception of the Church. While many of the houses date back three centuries or more, in Church Lane the old picturesque houses include Lychgate and Lychgate Cottage. In 1968, these were discovered to be rare surviving examples of medieval wealden houses. Horsfield, in *History of Sussex* mentions 'Linkwell', as it was later named, as 'one of the very handsome residences of Bexhill'; it was built in 1820 in the 'Italianate' style and remains little altered today. 'The Grange', formerly 'Brook Lodge', at the top of Upper Sea Road was for many years the home of that well-known family, while 'Linkwell' has been in the same family since it was built, passing down through the female line. The largest landowner in Bexhill in the second half of the 19th century, after the De La Warr family, was Samuel Scrivens, who lived at 'Millfield', Belle Hill. Formerly it was known as 'The Firs' and was acquired by Mr. Scrivens through marriage into the Bexhill landed family of Moorman.

In 1881 the opening of the Old Town home of the Metropolitan Convalescent Institution led to recognition of Bexhill as a health resort, and this fact subsequently led to much of the development of Hastings Road.

With the loss of the old walnut tree, which formerly stood at the junction, opposite the *Bell*, the most striking feature of the Old Town is the Jubilee Memorial Clock erected in 1887 to commemorate the first of Queen Victoria's jubilees. The clock continued to function until 1908 when the building in which it was housed was destroyed by fire. However, the external part was little damaged and, with the fitting of new works in the same year, the clock continued striking each hour for a further 80 years until 1969, when objection was raised by some residents concerning its striking bell during the night.

Whilst the Manor House has been demolished and little remains of the medieval buildings apart from a buttress and a trefoil-headed window, the ornamental gardens which include a walled garden, rose garden, lily pond and aviary are a delight. A Museum of Period Costume is housed in the Old Manor Library, one of the three buildings which still remain within the Manor House grounds. The other two are the Manor Barn and the Coach House. The Manor Barn, originally the Ballroom of the Manor House, was acquired for Bexhill in 1970. It is a beautifully-restored building with oak panelled and timbered interior. The Coach House, built about 1886, was, until 1965, used to house the servants who worked in the Manor House and grounds. From 1977 it was leased to the Servants with Jesus, a fellowship of ladies drawn from the different traditions of the Church. Barrack Hall at the other end of the High Street is now St. Jude's, a refuge for Battered Wives; thus the Old Town continues its reputation for the caring of those less fortunate.

One of the most outstanding developments since the Second World War has been the Community Association movement, of which the pioneer in Bexhill was Canon Godfrey Bell, Rector from 1941 to 1953. The St. Peter's Association was formed in 1946, using the two older church halls. In 1955 a new hall was built and a wide range of activities for people of all ages take place within these three buildings.

SIDLEY

In Saxon times, when most of Sussex was covered with forest, Sidley (or 'Sydelegh' to give it its original spelling) was nothing more than a clearing in the wood, which is what the name denotes.

Sidley (thought to be older than Bexhill itself) was formerly a hamlet on the high road inland from the ancient port of Bulverhythe on the direct route to Ninfield and beyond. Budgen's map of 1724 shows Bexhill only as an unattached crossroads, some distance south of this main road. Footpaths abounded, connecting otherwise isolated farms with the separated Bexhill, Little Common and Sidley communities, which retain their individualities to this day.

There were iron works in the area in the 16th and 17th centuries. There is evidence of an old bloomery at Sidley where the railway line used to run, and Buckholt had a forge and furnace. There was in existence by the 15th century a forge at Sidley, which closed in the 1950s having been worked for 500 years.

As the land was cleared it was cultivated; the parish still contains several farms, for the village itself grew to serve the farming community. The Ordnance Survey of 1813 showed three mills at Sidley, the last survivor of these being Pankhurst's Mill, which was purchased in 1928 for £25 by a lover of windmills, carefully taken down, and re-erected at Leigh, Kent, at a cost of £1,500 (L. P. Bartley, *The Story of Bexhill*, 1971, p. 95). Of the others, one was near Old Mill House, and east of the Ninfield Road, in a field suggested in 1884 for the first Bexhill Waterworks, stood Cumberland Mill. This mill is indicated on the Ordnance revision of 1873, but had disappeared by this century.

Sidley had two inns, the *New* Inn (thought to be over 500 years old), which throughout the centuries has been little altered, and the old *Sussex Beerhouse* opposite; the *Sussex* Hotel is today built on this latter site.

With the growth of the seaside resort of Bexhill-on-Sea, building advanced towards Sidley during the 1890s, but the chief expansion, and with it prosperity, came from the construction of the Bexhill West to Crowhurst branch line with a station at Sidley. Mr. J. P. Goodwin (a member of the Urban Council, and son of the proprietor of the old-established hostelry the *Queens Head*, in Belle Hill) built the *Pelham* Hotel in 1902 (opposite this station); he supported his application by the contention that there was no stabling to be had at Sidley and the hotel would provide stalls, loose boxes and carriage horses.

In 1865, at Sidley, then part of St. Peter's parish, was built a 'controlled' school for the education of 'poor children of both sexes, inhabitants of Sidley parish'. This building was also used for worship until the erection of the 'Iron' Church in 1885 (*The Story of Bexhill*, p. 84). A larger permanent structure was not built until 1909. However, Nonconformity had come to Sidley early; by 1840 the local preachers served their congregation in a carpenter's shop and in 1873 the cause at Sidley was encouraged by a small band of missionaries from the Primitive Methodist Church at Hastings to erect a tiny chapel in Haddocks Hill. Springfield Road Methodist Church was opened in 1907. The inhabitants of Sidley were not always tolerant of others practising their faith and the Ninfield Salvationists, who marched to Bexhill in the last century to hold meetings, were subjected to showers of refuse while passing through the village.

At Sidley, a band grew from an orchestra formed in the late 1870s at the Working Men's Club; early in the century it became the Bexhill Town Band. Another band which originally started as an orchestra became the Springfield Brass Band and the two merged into The Town Band after the First World War, continuing until the early 1950s.

As early as the 1890s cricket was played at Sidley but the present club dates from 1901. Bowls were and still are played at Sidley, and so is football; Sidley Club dates from before 1914.

Sidley in the last century had two blacksmith's forges (one owned by Turner's the other by Beal and Catt), and also a wheelwright's shop (owned and operated by the Beal family); now all are closed. There was also a local brickyard operated by the Adams family, many of whose hand-made bricks were used to build the rapidly-expanding village.

Municipal housing came to Sidley after the First World War with the development of Buxton Drive. Further dwellings were erected after the Second World War on the Ingrams Farm estate and at Southlands; shops opened in the neighbourhood to serve this growing community. Today this area of the town houses the youngest population group.

LITTLE COMMON AND COODEN

Little Common and Cooden lie west of the valley which separates the Old Town from Bexhill Down and the higher ground to the north; a low, undulating ridge extends to Barnhorn overlooking Pevensey marsh, with a southerly branch to Cooden Down. This area retained for centuries a greater affinity with the Pevensey Levels, both for reasons of geography and the separate lordship of its manors; Barnhorn was held by Battle Abbey for 400 years until the Reformation (L. P. Bartley, *The Story of Bexhill*, 1971, p. 2).

The name Little Common, now generally applied to the area, does not appear on Sussex maps until that of the Ordnance Survey dated 1813. In 1805 the *Sussex Weekly Advertiser* reported the murder of a soldier of the King's German Legion (stationed at Bexhill) whose body was found on a 'Little Common', a tract of land known for centuries as 'Slyder's Common' and which lay between Cooden Down and the present village (*The Story of Bexhill*, p. 2).

By 1800 Little Common had a big triangular green; common land used for grazing purposes. From this led cart-tracks; one to Cooden Down and the sea; another to Barnhorn; and one to Bexhill, which went through the present churchyard and passed Kewhurst House, then Lloyd's Signal Station. Across the green was the *Wheatsheaf* Inn, the oldest part of which is Tudor. In the village was a blacksmith's forge owned by the Crocker family and a wheelwright's shop belonging to the Dick family. The village pond served both with water.

Farming was the major occupation at Little Common but it did not pay as well as smuggling and the village had one of the best known smuggling gangs in East Sussex, led by the Gillham family, respectable builders and carpenters by day, smugglers by night.

Before 1842 there was no church, but in that year the first portion of St. Mark's was built, largely from material (it is said) from the No. 42 martello tower, which was demolished at Bulverhythe. This material was brought by sea to the beach at the bottom of Cooden Sea Lane (now Road) and thence transported by cart to the church site.

The 8th Earl De La Warr laid out the Cooden Golf Club in 1912 on the grounds belonging to old Cooden Manor. In the previous century martello tower No. 50 had stood there; it was demolished by the latest breech-loading guns then in use, under the watchful eye of the then Commander-in-Chief of the Army, The Duke of Cambridge. While the opening of the Golf Club gave Bexhill added prestige in the sporting world, equally important, it led to the making up of Cooden Drive along the tramway, which before this event ran from Bexhill to Cooden Beach through cornfields.

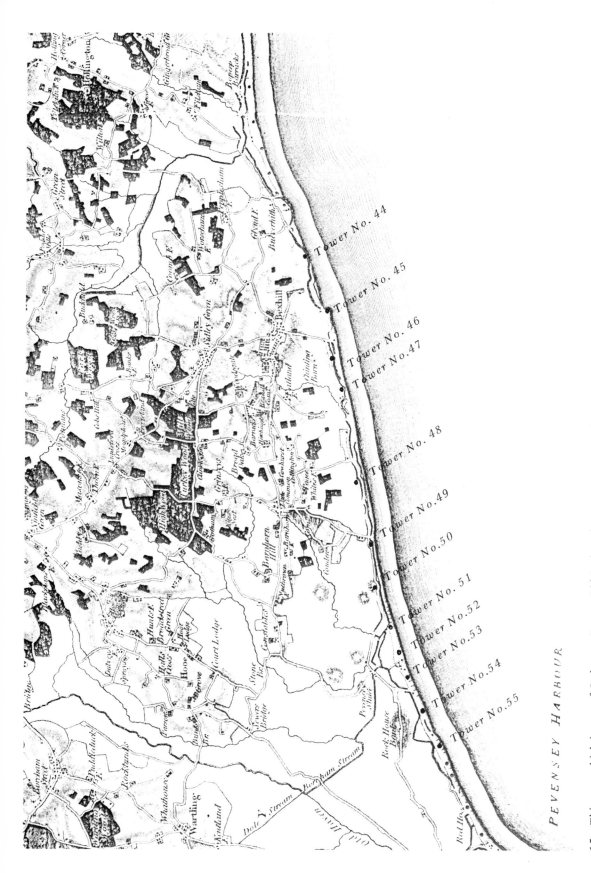

Tower No. 44
Tower No. 45
Tower No. 46
Tower No. 47
Tower No. 48
Tower No. 49
Tower No. 50
Tower No. 51
Tower No. 52
Tower No. 53
Tower No. 54
Tower No. 55

PEVENSEY HARBOUR

15. This map which is part of Ordnance Survey Old Series 1 in. map 1795-1825 shows the position of the twelve martello towers which stood along the foreshore from No. 44 at Galley Hill to No. 55 at Normans Bay. When tower No. 48 was erected, this altered the numbering westwards. No. 45 which stood south of where the *Sackville* Hotel was later built, had already disappeared due to erosion before 1839. No. 44 on Galley Hill was the only one of the towers in the parish to be surrounded by a moat. This portion of the map truly illustrates the rural nature of the village of Bexhill surrounded by farms before the beginning of the urban development.

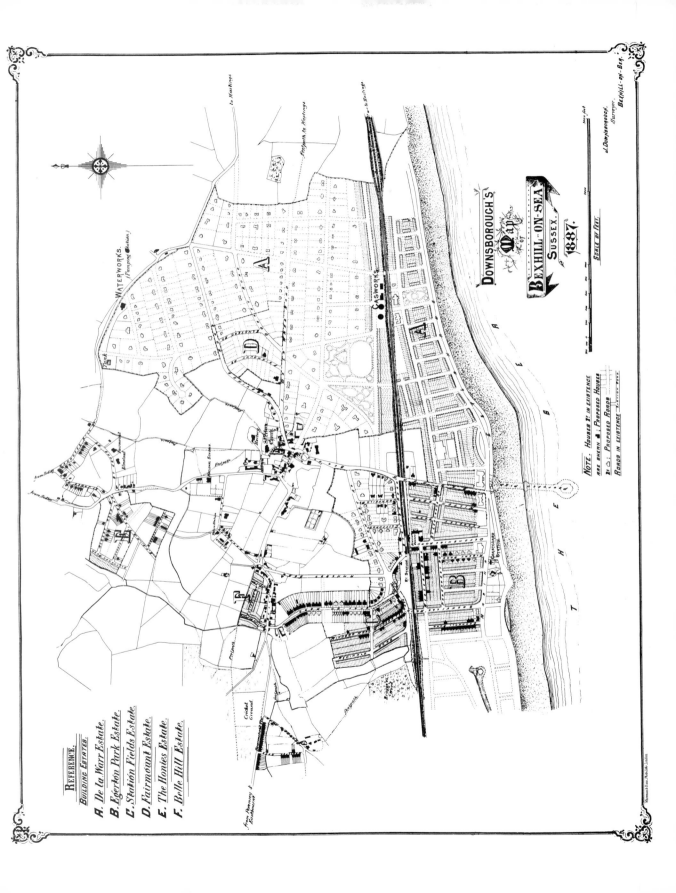

DOWNSBOROUGH'S
Map
OF
BEXHILL-ON-SEA
SUSSEX.
1887.

SCALE OF FEET.

J. Downsborough,
Surveyor,
Bexhill-on-Sea.

NOTE. Houses in existence
are shown ■; Proposed Houses
□; Proposed Roads
Roads in existence

REFERENCE.
BUILDING ESTATES.
A. De la Warr Estate.
B. Egerton Park Estate.
C. Station Fields Estate.
D. Fairmount Estate.
E. The Honies Estate.
F. Belle Hill Estate.

WATERWORKS.
(Pumping Station.)

GASWORKS.

Cricket Ground.

RESULT OF THE POLL.

THIS DAY.

BEXHILL DISTRICT COUNCIL ELECTION

ELECTED		NOT ELECTED	
Lane -	531	Atchison - -	169
Young - -	502	Prance -	150
Smith, S. -	493	Hicks -	125
Wallis -	401	Harmer -	101
Smith, W. -	385	Neve	90
Cantelupe - -	371	Price -	75
Greed - -	367	Ratcliff -	59
Gray - -	324	Ney - -	51
Duke - -	307	Wall -	47
Webb -	282		
Cooper -	260		
Vidler -	258		
Murrell - -	257		
Adams - -	251		
Dunn - -	219		

Five Spoilt Papers.

ELECTION OF BEXHILL GUARDIANS.

ELECTED		NOT ELECTED	
Egerton, Miss -	548	Jenner -	167
Noakes -	434	Dewing -	137
Oliver -	292		
Atchison -	278		
Cooper -	245		

16. (*Previous page*) Map of Bexhill-on-Sea by J. Downsborough dated 1887 shows the various estates which were being developed at this time, a key to which is in the left-hand top corner. It is interesting to note that the site of the proposed pier was opposite Sea Road; early in the next century it was proposed that Bexhill should have a pier opposite Devonshire Road. At this time, 1887, Bexhill had two Albert Roads, the existing one and another off Springfield Road now renamed Havelock Road. See 'E' the Honies Estate on map.

17. The placard which announced the result of Bexhill's first Urban Council election in December 1894. Also, the result of the local election that year for the Battle Board of Guardians, when Bexhill returned its first lady representative in local government, Miss C. A. Egerton.

18. Lieutenant-Colonel Henry Lane, 'father' of local government is best remembered today by his memorial in Town Hall Square. A veteran of the Indian Mutiny, he became the first chairman of the local Board, the first resident Justice of the Peace and chairman of the Urban Council. When the Local Government Act of 1888 created county councils, Bexhill was allowed one member on the East Sussex County Council and at the election in January 1889, Lt. Col. Henry Lane was the successful candidate. He later became the first county alderman from the town. He died in 1896.

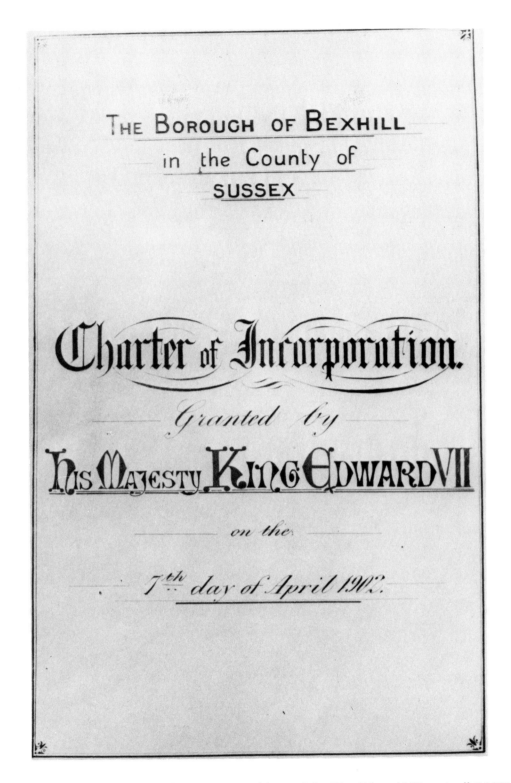

THE BOROUGH OF BEXHILL

in the County of

SUSSEX

Charter of Incorporation.

Granted by

His Majesty King Edward VII

on the

7th day of April 1902.

19. Bexhill was granted the status of an incorporated borough by King Edward VII on April 7 1902, but a petition for a charter had been made to Queen Victoria two years earlier. The town's reception of the charter remains an outstanding day in local history; the document was publicly read to a large crowd outside the Town Hall and a procession and other festivities followed. No town received a charter after Bexhill, consequently it became the youngest of the 10 boroughs in the county of Sussex.

FOOD PANIC.

—:o:—

UNPATRIOTIC CONDUCT IN BEXHILL.

RUSH FOR PROVISIONS CHECKED.

THE MAYOR'S APPEAL.

During the first three days of the week there was an alarming rush on the provision shops of the town. A number of residents, getting alarmed at the situation, and fearing, presumably, the imminence of a food famine, rushed to the shops and purchased large quantities of flour, sugar, tea, bacon, etc., with which to stock their houses. Grocers and their staffs were kept working night and day to cope with the orders. Remarkable scenes were witnessed at some of the stores, whose stocks became exhausted. Some shops had to close their doors temporarily. So serious did the situation be-

NATIONAL VOLUNTEERS.

—:o:—

Proposed Corps at Bexhill.

EARL DE LA WARR'S PATRIOTIC OFFER.

WAR OFFICE APPROACHED.

We have received the following important letter from Earl De La Warr:—

To the Editor of the "Bexhill Observer."

Sir,—The nation is involved in a War, the results and consequences of which no one can foresee. We are face to face with the fact that the services of every able-bodied Englishman may be required in the defence of his country. A large

NO TIME FOR FEAR.

—:o:—

Rector Suggests Prayers for the Navy.

NATIONAL ANTHEM TO BE SUNG KNEELING.

Yesterday we received the following communication from the Ven. Archdeacon Churton, Rector of Bexhill:—

To the Editor of the "Bexhill Observer."

Sir,—Though this is a time of grave anxiety, it cannot be a time of unworthy fear to those who know (for who can possibly doubt?) that the War that has been so suddenly thrust upon us, and with so brutal and elementary justice, is a war in which, with a clear conscience, and with strong confidence we may, as a United Empire, call upon Almighty God to "give strength unto His people," and so finally to 'give His people

20 & 21. Headlines from a local newspaper of August 1914 and reading the war news at the Colonnade. The first intimation of the imminence of war was when the band of the 15th Hussars was recalled to Aldershot from playing at the Colonnade. The patriotic fervour was offset by a rush for food-stuffs which necessitated an appeal by the Mayor, Alderman Daniel Mayer, for restraint. Although a naturalised Englishman, being of German extraction, Alderman Mayer resigned the mayoralty soon afterwards feeling that the townspeople would prefer a native of their country to be first citizen at such a time.

22. (*Opposite*) The front page of a local newspaper, *The Bexhill-on-Sea Chronicle,* 24 September 1887, first issue. The paper was acquired the next year by a newly formed local company and moved in 1893 to offices in Town Hall Square which it occupied for the remaining 37 years of its existence. It came under new proprietorship in 1911 and was taken over by *The Bexhill-on-Sea Observer* in 1930.

THE BEXHILL ON SEA CHRONICLE

AND VISITORS' LIST,

BATTLE, PEVENSEY, SIDLEY, AND LITTLE COMMON ADVERTISER.

No. 1. SATURDAY, SEPTEMBER 24, 1887. One Penny.

23. Beating Bexhill's Bounds, at the time of the incorporation of the borough in 1902. The boundary was marked out by 63 large stones spaced along the perimeter from Normans Bay on the west, Lunsfords Cross on the north of the town and Glyne Gap on the east. Stone No. 63 marked the boundary with Hastings county borough but it was washed away by the sea soon after it was erected. The ceremony of Beating the Bounds was carried out in 1905, 1925 and 1928 when the remaining 62 stones were traced. These inspections were notable for some jollity and members and officials of the Town Council were ceremonially 'bumped'. Unfortunately when an attempt was made in the golden jubilee year of the borough in 1952 to trace the stones marking the boundary, there were insufficient enthusiasts to volunteer to do this.

24. An unusual building which stood on the beach at Cooden until demolished in 1920, was a little shack. It was used as a look-out by the coastguard and was known in the neighbourhood as 'the Bricks'. This building was built of rubble from martello tower No. 50 which had been used for target practice in 1860.

25. St. Peter's church after the restoration of 1878. The church has a low embattled tower surmounted by a cap. The tower has Norman arches north and south and the two western bays of the nave arcades are late 12th century with round piers and round-headed arches; the piers have simple Norman capitals, scallops on the north, stylised leaves on the south. The next two bays on the north are early English and a perpendicular on the south, rebuilt by Butterfield in 1878. Some residents spoke with dismay of their much loved church being 'handed over to the tender mercy of Mr. Butterfield!'. The north chapel was founded in about 1450 as the Batesford chantry. In the north aisle is a window containing some 15th century glass with whole figures. The glass was acquired by Horace Walpole from the then rector in about 1750 and was used to adorn his villa at Strawberry Hill. After Walpole's death it was bought by Sir Thomas Cullum of Hardwick House, Bury St. Edmunds, and bequeathed to Bexhill church by his descendant in 1921. In 1893 the chancel ceiling was decorated and the walls painted. In 1906 the accommodation was further extended by the building of a new north aisle.

26. (*Below*) Drawing of the interior of St. Peter's church before the restoration of 1878.

27. (*Right*) Interior of St. Peter's church, west end, 1887 before the restoration the following year when the ugly galleries introduced in the 18th century were removed.

28. (*Left*) Interior view of St. Peter's church after the restoration.

The Smithy, Old Town, Bexhill.

29. (*Opposite*) The *Bell* Hotel was an ancient posting house and centre of village life and was improved in 1888 when the hotel was given its modern facade. Records show that the *Bell* had long been familiar to visitors who came to enjoy the countryside as well as the sea breezes. A directory for 1840 stated that Bexhill was an 'inconsiderable town in respect of trade, but is visited in the summer months by a few respectable families for the purpose of sea bathing, for whose accommodation there are machines on the beach'. The social life of Bexhill first centred on the *Bell* Hotel where an assembly room served as a theatre; it was also the venue for the Local Board before completion of the Town Hall.

30. (*Opposite below*) Interior of the Old Town forge about 1927-28. The man on the left of the picture is Mr. Wood and the one on the right, Mr. Jim Wimborne, the horse being shod was Billy who belonged to Pocock's the butchers in the High Street. The Pocock family opened their first butcher's shop and slaughter house in about 1770 and in 1801 moved into their present premises.

31. Drawing of the Old Town forge by C. Graves. On the opposite side of the road is one of the entrances of the Manor House Estate, the house shown being South Lodge, demolished in 1968. This forge was operating until the Second World War but was finally pulled down in 1947.

32. The Manor House. In medieval times the Manor was a seat of the
Bishops of Chichester, but by the 18th century it had become a shooting
lodge for the Dorset family, the Lords of the manor, who came for wild-
fowling over the marshes, now covered by much of the modern town.
In the 19th century it was occupied as a farmhouse by, among others,
the well-known Brook family. The Manor was altered in 1891 for
Viscount Cantelupe. The ancient part of the house was incorporated
into additions of good taste, including a large bay-windowed drawing
room. Outbuildings were erected, an electricity supply, powered by a
gas engine, and a private telephone service installed between the house
and the estate buildings. The whole restoration was stated to have cost
up to £15,000. Lord and Lady Cantelupe moved in, in August 1892,
celebrating the occasion with a lavish house-warming which included
the entertainment of 160 guests, followed by a ball for 200 of the principal residents of Bexhill and the estate staff. Until the South African
War the Manor House was a centre of the fashionable weekend house
parties of the period and many distinguished visitors, including royalty,
were entertained. Later occupants following Viscount Cantelupe were
Neven du Mont, son of a Cologne publisher, who was for a time master
of the East Sussex foxhounds, and Sir Leicester Harmsworth, (brother
of Lord Northcliffe) who possessed a magnificent library. His widow
remained at the Manor House until her death in 1963. The Manor
House was subsequently bought by the Bexhill Corporation for
£23,000 in 1963 and demolished. However, some of the ruins,
including a buttress and a trefoil-headed window remain, together
with certain outbuildings and the old walled garden.

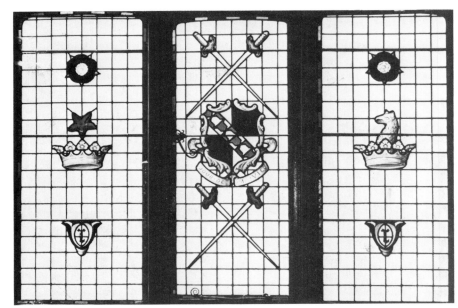

33. This window which was formerly in the Chapel Room of the demolished Manor House, showed the De La Warr Arms, with the family motto 'Jour de ma Vie' (Day of my Life) in the centre light and on either side, the crests which surmount the arms.

34. A photograph of the High Street, Old Town, c. 1890 shows clearly Hibberd the Chemist and the shop of Pocock the butcher next door to Boswell House owned by this family. The cottage fourth from the left was demolished in the last century and may be seen more clearly in picture No. 35.

35. High Street, Bexhill Old Town looking eastwards. On the left may be seen the old chemists shop, now the Beehive and next door, Pocock's butcher shop. Drawing by C. Graves.

36. Church Street before 1870. On the left will be seen the *Bell* Hotel which was renovated in 1888. In the background, part of St. Peter's church and on the right-hand side of the road, a cottage now known as 'Lychgate'. In 1968 it was discovered that this house nearest the church was one of only two of its type known in England to archaeologists as a 'wealden house'. An 18th century or early 19th century brick facade disguises this fact, but early in its history, the house was typical of its period. It was dominated by a single large hall extending from floor to rafters. In a demonstration of communal living that would today seem strange, every occupant shared this single room dominated by a vast fireplace. At the front there would have been a prominent overhang or 'jetty'. A second 'jetty' probably ran along one side. At the rear ran a passageway known as an 'aisle'. Despite their different frontages, adjoining properties, in particular that known as Lychgate Cottage, may be mirror images of the hall house. However, many of these properties are clad in weather-boarding and centuries of alteration and extension cloak their true origins.

37. Church Street from St. Peter's churchyard Old Town, Bexhill. Drawing by C. **Graves**, 1898.

38. On 20 June 1908, the warehouse belonging to Cave Austin and Company, grocers, with premises in the Old Town, was gutted by fire. Both the building and the Jubilee clock which had been erected by public subscription, were destroyed. A replica was made and ceremonially started on King Edward's birthday the same year. Today this clock may still be seen keeping excellent time on the same building which is now an antique centre.

39. Looking across Pevensey marshes to Beachy Head in the distance, a picture painted by Francis Grose on the occasion of his visit to Bexhill in 1787. It is thought that the flat roofed buildings shown here in Belle Hill may be part of the garrison buildings erected here prior to those constructed for the King's German Legion during the Napoleonic Wars.

40 & 41. Two interesting views of the old walnut tree which for many years was a feature of the Old Town. In the first photograph c. 1888, the tree stands behind the wall of the Manor House, whereas in the second picture c. 1905, the tree is in the centre of the road, the wall has been demolished and a wooden fence erected instead. The stump of the tree was removed in 1921 and a gavel made from it was used by the 9th Earl De La Warr at the laying of the commemorative stone on the occasion of the opening of the Town Hall extension. The clock shown in photograph No. 38 was erected in 1887 to mark the occasion of the first of Queen Victoria's Jubilees.

BEXHILL. OLD WALNUT TREE.

42. This small Belle Hill chapel was built on land which had formed part of the King's German Legion depot during the Napoleonic Wars. The Wesleyans bought it from the Government in 1825 and erected this building. The chapel was served by local preachers 'on the plan', first from Lewes, then Hastings from the 1820s, with the appointment of a minister to that town. From the Belle Hill missionary enterprises began Wesleyan fervour at Little Common in 1837 and in a carpenters shop at Sidley three years later.

HIGH STREET BEXHILL

C.K

43. (*Far left*) High Street, Old Town c. 1900 looking westwards, a view little altered today. Barrack Hall, for a time used as officers quarters for the King's German Legion during the Napoleonic Wars, lies behind the trees in the distance. 'Linkwell' an Italianate villa built c. 1830 is set back behind the trees on the left of the picture.

44. (*Above*) The Grand Ducal party at the Bexhill cycle tournament in 1897. Sitting second from the left is the Grand Duke Michael of Russia and third from the left is his wife, Countess de Torby. Behind them stands Earl De La Warr, and others included are the Reverend E. Mortlock, first vicar of St. Barnabas' church; next to him is Dr. J. P. Wills, and beside him in a boater, Mr. C. A. Egerton.

45. (*Left*) Official Programme relating to the cycling tournament promoted by the Rt. Hon. Earl De La Warr in the Manor House grounds, Bexhill, August bank holiday, 1897.

46. (*Right*) These old cottages were erected during the time of the Napoleonic Wars and used by the King's German Legion. Later in the century, the building became the Wilson Memorial School until it was incorporated into St. Peter's school in Barrack Road, which opened in 1885.

47. (*Below*) Belle Hill, Bexhill. Drawing by C. Graves, 1898.

48. (*Opposite below*) Another view of Belle Hill. The wooden cottage on the right has been demolished but it was erected at the time that the German troops were stationed in Bexhill, and was for their use and occupation, c. 1890. Drawing by C. Graves.

49 & 50. Herbert Pulham founded the Engineering firm of H. Pulham and Co. of Sackville Road and was a notable figure in pioneering methods. He ran motor trips, and in 1913 experimented with a Daimler double-decker omnibus which unfortunately proved too high to go under the Sackville arch. The second picture shows one of the Hallford chain-drive double-decker omnibuses taken over by the Maidstone and District when the Company was formed in 1911.

51 & 52. Two views of Chantry Lane looking northwards, taken in 1928. Today this vista is lost for all time due to the Bexhill Old Town by-pass flyover road passing overhead. Generations of children have enjoyed clambering up the slippery banks of this road.

Chantry Lane, Bexhill

53. (*Above*) The Australian Cricketing team. In 1893 Viscount Cantelupe laid out a private cricket ground where he entertained the South African tourists in 1894, and two years later, the Australian Test team, the most famous match in local history. This ground was later cut up to make **Magdalen and Manor Roads in 1898** and Lord De La Warr (formerly Viscount Cantelupe) laid out a second ground adjoining Dorset Road, which is now part of St. Richard's school playing fields.

54. (*Opposite below*) Mr. Edward Mason of Belmont Dairy, Sidley, in his milk float at the top of Chantry Lane in 1915. This dairy was founded by Mr. Ottonay in 1899 and taken over by W. H. Marten in 1922.

55. (*Right*) In the past, many windmills stood on the high ground to the north of the town; today only the brick roundels of the Down Mill at Glenleigh Park and of Pankhurst's Mill at Sidley remain as evidence. The most celebrated mill was the Down, erected in 1735. Acquired by the Hoad family in 1857, it continued working until 1928 and finally collapsed in 1965.

56. This picture shows Thomas Hoad (in the cart) uncle to Mr. Clifford Hoad who, with his son, today still bakes bread on this site. The young lady was Millie Eastwood, (Eastwood Road, previously Braggs Lane was named after her father, Ben). Unfortunately, it has been impossible to identify the two other people. It is interesting to note that Mr. Clifford Hoad also had a road named after him in the developing seaside resort.

57. (*Previous page*) The original Ancaster House class of 1906 with their founding principal Mrs. Burrows. The two young ladies on either side of her were her daughters and it was the elder, Frances, who was appointed headmistress, an office she held for 46 years. The style and tradition of Ancaster House owes much to the spirited leadership of Miss Burrows, whose influence on the town extended far beyond the confines of the school itself.

58 (*Below*) & **59.** (*Opposite top*) Two pictures showing the old pond at Little Common. Children fishing for tiddlers during the spring and summer months and enjoying sliding and skating in the winter. In the background may be seen the *Wheatsheaf* Inn. During the winter months, the pond was known to overflow and on many occasions flooded the cottages opposite.

60. (*Opposite*) Little Common pond, showing clearly the village blacksmith's house and forge where Mr. Crocker used to carry on his trade, also the village green and pond. Close by was Mr. Dick's wheelwright shop. The pond was often used for watering cattle, the rails being open at both ends.

61. (*Opposite below*) Local children dancing around a maypole at the Little Common Flower Show on 24 July 1912.

LITTLE COMMON POND & WHEATSHEAF INN.

MAYPOLE DANCE LITTLE COMMON FLOWER SHOW JULY 24TH 1912. 155 E

HELLIER. BEXHILL

690—COODEN SEA ROAD, LITTLE COMMON.

62. Cooden Sea Road, Little Common, looking southwards.

1591. Sea Road, Little Common, Bexhill-on-Sea.

63. Cooden Sea Road, Little Common, looking northwards, a photograph taken in the 1920s shows the War memorial which still stands at the cross-roads.

W. SHEPHERD & SONS
Road Contractors
ROCHDALE

64. Sackville Road, c. 1924. In the distance is the railway bridge. This was modernised for a cattle arch in 1892 and again widened in 1920. It will be seen that the lamp posts, like those in Devonshire Road, were in the centre of the road. Many of the main streets of Bexhill were planted with trees, few of which remain today.

WIMSHURST'S SEVEN CURES.

CORN CURE, 7½ and 1/- *Never Fails.*

COUGH CURE, 1/- and 2 9 *Very Useful.*

COLD & INFLUENZA CURE, 1/- *Always Effectual.*

CHOLERA & DIARRHŒA CURE, 1/- *Certain Relief.*

NEURALGIA CURE, 1/- *Safe Speedy Cure.*

TOOTHACHE CURE, 7½ and 1/- *Magic in its Use.*

INDIGESTION CURE, 1/-.—*Quick Relief.*

WIMSHURST'S CANTHARIDINE HAIR WASH,
1 - Double Size, 1/6. Imp. Pint, 3/0.
Is unequalled for promoting the growth of the Hair.

WIMSHURST'S EXCELSIOR SKIN SOAP   4½d. per Cake
Especially suited for the Bexhill Water. Try a Cake and
you'll always use it.

WIMSHURST'S GLYCERINE and CUCUMBER   6d. and 1/-
For Summer's Heat, and Winter's Winds. An excellent preparation for Chapped Hands, and bad effects of the weather.

WIMSHURST'S THROAT LOZENGES   -   -   1/-
Invaluable to Public Speakers. Removes all Irritation
and Soreness of the Throat.

ALL GENUINE PREPARATIONS,
Well-tried and proved to be of Value.

65. (*above*) The wheelwrights pre 1914. At this time the building was thought to be over 100 years old and said to have been used originally as a stable for the horses which drew the stagecoach on the Brighton - Hastings run. Accommodation was provided for the ostlers and stable boys in the loft overhead. It was acquired by George Dicks senior in 1859. In 1861 the loft was used by men of the Royal Horse Artillery while on gunnery practice in which they demolished martello tower No. 50 at Cooden.

66. (*Left*) Wimshurst's Seven Cures. Many of the early Property Registers prepared by the local Estate Agents carried advertisements for various products stocked by the shops in the town. Most of these items were prepared on the premises and promised practically instant cures for almost every ailment!

67. (*Overleaf*) 'Taking the air' at Little Common. A picture showing the crossroads and the village pond, c. 1910.

LITTLE COMMON VILLAGE 234A

HELLIER, BEXHILL

68. Elliot's Stores, Little Common, photographed in 1936 after it had finally closed, following the death of Mr. Ted Elliott. This store was founded in the days of Napoleon and the business of 'grocers, drapers, chandlers and ironmongers' was carried on by the Stride family. Records show that in 1818 the business was owned by a Mr. Richard Stride who was then selling groceries to Mr. George Gillham, leader of the Little Common gang of smugglers. A grocery account of 1818 shows that Richard was selling a wide variety of goods but not wines and spirits, probably for the very good reason that the Gillhams were doing very well illicitly in that line of business themselves! About 1880 Elliott's Stores passed into the hands of Mr. Richard Elliott who was related to Richard Stride.

69. (*Above*) A self-explanatory photograph of the annual outing of the Ninfield Mission Hall Sunday School to Little Common, June 1898, seen outside the *Wheatsheaf* Inn where the original of this photograph hangs today.

70. (*Left*) Unveiling of the Little Common War Memorial, 21 November 1920. Elliott's store is on the left of the picture. This unveiling was marked by the first official attendance of the Mayor and Corporation and they are standing to the right of the officiating clergy.

71. (*Left*) Mittens old house, c. 1900. This cottage originally stood in Ocklynge Close, Pear Tree Lane, Little Common. Mary Mitten lived in this house and died in 1897 one week short of 101.

72. (*Overleaf*) The Harriers' meet on the green at Little Common, the road in the background being Church Hill, 1912. The hounds, the 'Black and Tans', were quite famous and many distinguished folk, including Edward VII when Prince of Wales, enjoyed a good days hunting with this pack. Both Earl De La Warr and Lord Brassey were masters in their time.

HARRIERS

MEET. LITTLE COMMON.   JAN. 1ST 1912.

HELLIER, BEXHILL.

73. (*Left*) Little Common had two
Inns, the *Wheatsheaf* beside the
green, originally an old posting
house and the *Denbigh* Hotel on
the hill half a mile east of the
village.

74. (*Below*) In 1908 an Orchestra was formed to accompany the singing of the Sidley Brotherhood, a popular men's
society, which started at the Methodist Church, now known as Springfield Road church; this eventually became the
Springfield Brass Band, and after the First World War, merged with the Town Band. The picture was taken in 1911.

75. (*Opposite top*) Sidley Infants School with the headmistress, Mrs. Kimber, in 1918. Many of the children are
still alive today. Sidley, at one time part of St. Peter's parish, had a controlled school in All Saints' Lane. It opened
in 1865 for the education of 'poor children of both sexes, inhabitants of Sidley Green in the parish of Bexhill and
other parts of the parish'. The building was also used for worship until the erection of the 'Iron' church in 1885.

76. (*Below*) Mr. John Beal and his six sons, all members of All Saints' church choir, taken in 1921. On the left of the picture, seated, is Mr. Cyril Beal who entered the service of the church as an eight year old choirboy at the beginning of the century and has served in this choir continuously for 80 years. For no less than 30 years of that time he was organist and choirmaster, a truly remarkable record of service.

SIDLEY, Bexhill-on-Sea.

Particulars and Conditions of Sale

The Sidley Brickyard,

1 and 2, Albert Villas,

1 and 2, Lewes Lass Cottages,

1, 2 & 3, Laburnham Cottages,

1, 2, and 3, Willow Cottages,

All at SIDLEY. BEXHILL-ON-SEA.

AND ALSO OF A

Plot of Freehold Building Land

Upon THE HONIES ESTATE,
BEXHILL-ON-SEA.

WHICH

MESSRS.

WOODHAMS & SON

Will Sell by Auction, at the

"BELL HOTEL," BEXHILL,

ON

Wednesday, May 2nd, 1900,

At FOUR o'clock in the Afternoon precisely.

A. NEVE, ESQ.,
SOLICITOR,
NORMAN ROAD, ST. LEONARDS.

T. H. WOODHAMS & SON,
AUCTIONEERS,
50, HAVELOCK ROAD, HASTINGS.

77. (*Above*) Mr. John Beal outside his engineering works adjacent to the Beal Catt forge, Sidley, c. 1920; with him are two of his six sons, Cyril and Reg. Mr. Will Smart stands by the door of the forge.

78. (*Left*) An advertisement relating to the sale of the Sidley Brickyard, Lewes Lass Cottages and other properties in the locality. 1900.

79. (*Opposite top*) Workers at the Adams Brickworks, Sidley, c. 1900. The outdoor nature of most local industry placed it at the mercy of the weather and seasonal unemployment which, in days when there was no social security, was all too common.

80. (*Opposite*) The *Sussex* Inn, Sidley. An old Sussex beerhouse stood in the High Street almost opposite the *New* Inn. On this site today stands the *Sussex* Hotel constructed at the turn of the century, c. 1890.

81. One of the seven engines which were used in the construction of the Bexhill West to Crowhurst Line, with a view of the workmen and their ganger (in bowler hat) grouped in front. Six of the engines bore local names and this one, the *Hastings*, was previously called *Nelson*. The picture was taken in 1902 in the cutting where Sidley station was built.

82. Photograph of Mrs. Sinden taken outside her cottage in Sidley, c. 1912. For many years this lady acted as village nurse and midwife to the community, and her reputation was such that at no time did she ever refuse her help when needed.

83. The wheelwright, John Beal, c. 1910. It was he who also owned the forge in Sidley High Street. In this picture he is seen on the left with Mr. Pettit and Mr. Cruttenden.

84. An early picture of the *New* Inn, Sidley, c. 1890, before the trees were planted on the green. On the left of the photograph is the *Sussex* beerhouse, now the *Sussex* Hotel.

85. Mr. W. B. Warner outside his hairdressing saloon in North Road, Sidley in 1925: as can be seen he sold a wide variety of goods. His assistant is possibly Mr. George Cole and the schoolgirl, who is still alive, is Mrs. Frank Fuller, previously Ivy Perry, whose family lived in Sidley for a number of years.

86. High Street, Sidley, early this century. On the right of the picture is the cottage belonging to Mrs. Clara Belle Eagling, one room of which was used by Lloyds Bank Ltd. In the centre of the picture is the Beal Catt forge and adjoining cottage.

89. *(opposite below)* Motor racing came to Bexhill on Whit-Monday 1902 with trials organised by the Automobile Club in conjunction with Earl De La Warr. The course ran from Galley Hill, shown in this picture, to the De La Warr Parade. Among the 200 competitors was Alfred Harmsworth, founder of the *Daily Mail*, and it was he who did much to popularise motoring. His younger brother, Leicester, bought the Manor House and estate later in the century. Unfortunately, a Parade resident whose access to his house was restricted by the racing, secured an injunction against such events. No further meeting was possible until 1904 when the times track was altered to omit that section. Bexhill ceased to be a venue for motor racing trials with the opening of the famous Brooklands tracks.

87. (*Left*) Mrs. Undecimus Stratton, wife of Daimler's London manager, at the wheel of her decorated car which won first prize at Bexhill's motor carnival, August bank holiday, 1904, a joint attraction with the three-day races held on East and De La Warr Parades.

88. (*Below*) Bexhill motor parade on the sea-front opposite the *Sackville* Hotel in 1902.

90. An early view of Egerton Park, beside the lake, c. 1890. Mr. John Webb who built the East Parade wall in 1883 was responsible for developing much of the town centre west of Sea Road and for the laying out of Egerton Park, which was taken over by the Urban Council at the turn of the century.

91. *Opposite*) Various activities took place in Egerton Park, bowls, tennis, band concerts and later in the century, a shelter hall was built for indoor performances, Jack Hulbert being among the artistes who appeared there. The hall is now the museum.

92. (*Above*) The second railway station at Bexhill was situated at the top of Devonshire Road, in what was then known as Station Square, south of the line. Bexhill previously had a station on the north side of the line (see photograph No. 7) long before Hastings. As the London, Brighton & South Coast Railway, opened in 1846, ran through much of the De La Warr Estate, the then Earl insisted that all trains should stop at Bexhill in order to serve the Old Town on the hill. The large building on the right is the *Devonshire* Hotel, c. 1891.

93. (*Right*) Children watching a game of tennis in Egerton Park.

94. (*Right*) A photograph showing the Peace Pageant which took place on 19 July 1919. The parade is approaching Sackville Arch.

95. (*Below*) The Cooden to Hastings trolley buses passing one another at Glyne Gap; the rails here ran through fields to Bulverhythe rather than follow the road where there was a precipitous bend and elevation towards the *Bull* Inn, c. 1920.

96. (*Opposite*) Secondary Education comes to Bexhill on 4 February 1927 with the opening of the two adjoining schools at Turkey Road. These schools were built to serve children coming from a wide area and were planned for 200 of each sex. The school was under the jurisdiction of the County Council and pupils had been in attendance since October 1926. In his opening speech, the chairman of governors said that the 'reason for building the school was that children might have a thorough education and that the need for higher educational facilities of this kind had been felt for years and would probably have been met but for the war'. Previously, children who wanted higher education had to travel to schools at Rye, Lewes, Eastbourne and Hastings, quite considerable distances.

In the picture from left to right: Colonel Sutherland Harris, chairman of governors; Lady Sargent; Miss E. Davis, M.A., Headmistress of the Girls' school; Mr. W. L. Lamb, M.A., Headmaster of the Boys' school; Sir Alfred Sargent, chairman of the County Council. Slightly in front of the group, the Duchess of Atholl, Parliamentary Secretary to the Board of Education and the only woman to hold office under the government at this time.

97. De La Warr Parade c. 1900 showing the Kursaal and Bandstand. Demand for seaside entertainment led Viscount Cantelupe to engage the White Viennese Band of Herr Stanislaus Wurm in 1849 to give concerts on the De La Warr Parade. So successful was this first summer season in the town's history that Wurm was given a contract until the end of the century. In the 19th century the bandstand was removed to a site in Egerton Park but, like the Kursaal, was subsequently demolished.

98. (*Right*) The 8th Earl De La Warr was responsible for building the Kursaal, a pier-like structure and pavilion which jutted seawards from the De La Warr parade. The Kursaal was never completed according to the original plans but it was opened on Whit-Monday 1896 by the popular Duchess of Teck, mother of the future Queen Mary. For many years the Kursaal remained the town's principal seat of entertainment and many famous artistes appeared there. In 1908 the Kursaal was sold by Earl De La Warr and thereafter gradually declined. Renamed the Pavilion during the First World War because of objection to the German name, it was eventually bought by the Corporation and in 1936 it was finally demolished, the site now being used by the Bexhill Sailing Club. The place of entertainment thus became the De La Warr Pavilion.

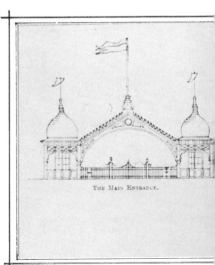

THE MAIN ENTRANCE.

THE KURSAAL,

EARL DE LA WARR'S ESTATE,

BEXHILL=ON=SEA,

Director - - - J. M. GLOVER.

SEASON 1901-02.

SUBSCRIBER'S BAND TICKET No. 208

October 1st to March, 1902.

ADMIT

Mr. George Brisley

TO THE KURSAAL,

READING & WRITING ROOMS

AND

ALL PERFORMANCES OF THE DE LA WARR ORCHESTRA ALONE. BUT NOT TO THEATRICAL OR OPERATIC PERFORMANCES.

This Ticket is transferable to members of the same family only (if presented by any person other than a member of the family to which it is issued, permission may be refused) and must at all times be produced on demand, and is issued on the condition that the holder shall abide by the rules and regulations of the Kursaal, made for subscribers' convenience.

Bexhill Printing Co., Ltd.

99. (*Left*) A ticket issued to Mr. George Brisley for the season 1901-1902 entitling him to all performances of the Orchestra and to the use of the Kursaal reading and writing rooms. A guide book for the same period states that 'in the morning and afternoon, high class orchestral performances are given'. Mr. J. M. Glover, whose signature appears on the ticket, was licensee of the Kursaal for some years. He was famous as musical director of Drury Lane Theatre. A great publicist with many friends in London newspaper circles, he did much to promote the interest of Bexhill in influential quarters. In some eight years at the Kursaal, 'Jimmy' Glover arranged over two thousand concerts.

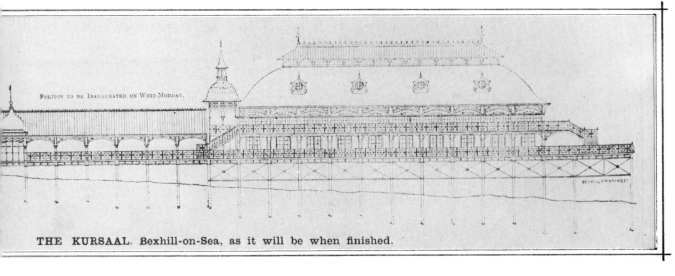

PORTION TO BE INAUGURATED ON WHIT-MONDAY.

THE KURSAAL, Bexhill-on-Sea, as it will be when finished.

100. The Kursaal and ornamental gates to the parade which formed part of the De La Warr Estate. From 1895 until

they were demolished in 1913; these gates could be shut to vehicular traffic.

H.R.H. The Duchess of Teck and H.S.H. The Duke of Teck

AT THE MANOR HOUSE.

101. The Kursaal was opened with great ceremony on Whit-Monday 1896 by the popular Duchess of Teck who with her husband were the guests of the Earl and Countess De La Warr on this occasion. The infant in the picture is Lady Myra Sackville, the eldest child of the De La Warr's.

102. The Bexhill Players, founded by Jack Fowler. Known as 'Uncle Jack' he was a popular entertainer of young holiday visitors and produced a wide range of musical and straight plays between the two World Wars.

103. (*Below*) During the summer of 1913 the Eastbourne Aviation Co. Ltd. ran a series of waterplane passenger flights from the beach in front of the Colonnade.

104. (*above*) Demolition of Sackville
Road Cattle Arch, 1892. Before the
parade embankments were built, the
first in 1883, the lower reaches of
modern Bexhill were marsh or swamp-
lands providing rough grazing. In 1927
W. H. Mullens, a High Sheriff of Sussex
and Mayor of Bexhill, recorded that
there were men still living who had
shot wildfowl where the Town Hall
now stands. With the construction of
the London Brighton and South Coast
Railway in 1846, cutting off this valuable marshland south of the line, it
was necessary to provide 'cattle arches'
for access to these lands. There were
four of these arches within the boundaries of the town, one at Cooden Beach,
one south of Collington Woods at
Westcourt Drive, the most important
one at Sackville Road, and one at
Glynde Gap (Bulverhythe).

105. (*opposite below*) The cattle arch leading from Cooden Drive to Westcourt Drive, c. 1921. As will be seen most of the land south of the railway line was marsh and little used except for the grazing of cattle in summertime.

106. (*below*) A number of bathing machines was in regular use in the lee of 'the Horn'. In 1911 the cliff was cut back to form a semi-circular gallery and the Colonnade erected thereon, c. 1890.

107. (*Above*) The distinctive Cycle Chalet on the De La Warr parade opposite the Sackville Hotel. This was used to store the machines for hire which were used on the cycle track constructed by the 8th Earl De La Warr in 1896 when the cycling boom was at its peak.

108. (*Opposite top*) The East Parade, the original part of which had been the first sea defence works to be constructed along the parish foreshore, was the last to come under municipal control. Until then it continued to be in the care of the De La Warr Estate which had developed it considerably with the fashionable expansion of the town in that area. The cycle track which was later used for the famous motor races, the Kursaal, the attractive gardens and the proximity of fine hotels, all combined to give the East Parade a status that was entirely distinctive, making it an exclusive promenade divided by the ornamental gates at the bottom of Sea Road. In the distance may be seen the chimney of the Ashdown Road Gas Works, now closed.

109. Preparation for war - local lads from the 230 Battery Royal Artillery filling sandbags on the beach opposite the *Normanhurst* Hotel, 1939. From left to right: Norman Cook; David Herring; unknown soldier; Alf Reynolds.

110. Procession of the Earl De La Warr's triumphant return from the Boer War passing along Devonshire Road where many of the local shops were especially decorated for this occasion.

111. (*Left*) Mr. William Gordon Harris and his sister, Harriet, outside his shop at 24 Station Road, celebrating the return of Viscount Cantelupe from the Boer War, 1900.

112. (*Below*) Western Road looking westwards, c. 1900. In the picture is one of the South Eastern and Chatham railway vans.

113. (*Opposite top*) Whilst the buildings are little changed today, it is impossible to imagine tea being taken in the open air, particularly as Bexhill is renowned for her breezy weather. This road was formerly known as East Pier Avenue, when it was contemplated that a pier would be built south of Devonshire Road.

114. (*Opposite*) Sketches of the opening of the New Municipal Building by the Lord Mayor of London, April 1895.

The Farm

The Reception before Luncheon

Municipal Building

115. (*above*) The opening of the Town Hall in 1895. In this picture may be seen the Mayor of Bexhill and his Town Clerk and attendants and on his left, the Lord Mayor.

116. (*Left*) A picture of the Town Hall taken soon after it opened in 1895. The building was designed by Mr. Henry Ward of Hastings, and the opening ceremony was performed by the Lord Mayor of London, Sir Joseph Renals, who at the invitation of Lord Cantelupe came in state with the sheriffs and the Lord Mayor's coach. An elaborate procession through the town made the day one of the most spectacular in local history, commemorated by a plaque inside the main entrance of the building.

117. **This** advertisement appeared in the supplement to the *Bexhill-on-sea Observer* dated Saturday 25 November 1899. In 1895 Viscount Cantelupe and Mr. R. Kersey applied for an electricity undertaking licence (this was later acquired by the Urban Council), and in 1900 the electricity undertaking started, when electric light was first switched on in Bexhill in April of that year. The claim was made that the town was one of the first in the country to supply electricity for domestic purposes.

BEXHILL-ON-SEA: THE CENTRAL PARA

BEXHILL-ON-SEA: WEST PARADE.

118 & 119. Two views of the sea front, Bexhill. The one of the Central Parade is much altered today with the demolition of Roberts Marine Mansions and Marine Court. The picture of the West Parade shows the front of the Metropole Hotel, looking westwards. At the waters edge may be seen the bathing machines and also some private beach huts, c. 1908.

120. (*Left*) View from the Old Town, Bexhill, c. 1870, looking towards the martello towers.

121. (*Below*) The Colonnade was completed in commemoration of the Coronation of King George V in 1911 and it was opened with great ceremony in the July of that year by Earl Brassey. The low cliff was cut back to form a semicircular gallery, open on the seaward side excepting in inclement weather, when by movable glass screens, it could be transformed into an indoor place of entertainment. The roof, level with the top of the cliff, formed a terrace, terminated at each end by a small dome. Originally, a semicircular widening of the parade, supported on piers over the beach, completed the circle, but this was destroyed later this century by the sea. The original scheme included a bandstand in the centre, and concerts and other entertainments were held throughout the season.

122. (*Opposite*) An early print of London Road, formerly known as Station Road, shows buildings still familiar today; however, the unmade footpath was typical of many in the town at that time.

EDGAR STREETS,
BOOKSELLER & STATIONER
CIRCULATING LIBRARY.
PIANO-FORTES
FOR SALE AND HIRE.

123. (*Below*) Chalybeate Spring, 1906, at the junction of London and St. George's Roads. John Walker built the well which is no longer there but the spring still runs, and the water is reputed to be similar to that at Tunbridge Wells. Two of the boys are Jack Neve and John Shoesmith and the biggest one is thought to be Victor Veness.

124. (*Below*) The 'bad old days' of the pre-war industrial depression taken in 1931, the year of the May Report, the fall of the second Labour Government, a sensational general election and the formation of a National Government in which Ramsey MacDonald was Prime Minister in a predominantly Conservative House of Commons. The photograph was taken outside the old Ministry of Labour office in Belle Hill and shows Salvation Army officers distributing welcome hot drinks to the waiting men. The notice in the window is dated October 1931, and gives details of unemployment benefit available.

125, 126 & 127. (*Opposite*) Bexhill has always suffered extensive damage from the sea and during 1912 a series of gales damaged the Colonnade deck and lifted coping stones along the Central Parade, besides creating other havoc along the East and West Parades. The second and third pictures show the same scene on a more peaceful occasion; the large building on the right is 'Oceania', for many years the only building on the sea front west of the *Metropole* Hotel, and behind it, the old Bandstand which finally succumbed during another gale in the 1960s. The Clock Tower, a prominent feature on the West Parade is the town's memorial to King Edward VII.

128, 129 & 130. The village green, Little Common, c. 1910. In the background of the first photograph may be seen Crockers the blacksmith and on the right, a corner of the *Wheatsheaf* Inn. The second and third photographs show details of the first.

131. A view much altered today showing the site of the Cooden Beach Golf Club north-west of this cottage and tea garden, now demolished. In the distance is the Men's Metropolitan Home, c.1910.

132. The celebration of the 25th anniversary of Charter Day which took place on 20 July 1927. The procession is passing along Marina.

133. One of the most popular social and sporting events is the annual Horse Show. First held in 1903, it originally included a parade of tradesmen's and other horse-drawn turn-outs, which processed through the streets of the town before arriving on the East Parade for the final judging.

134. The Bandstand and Marine Mansions, De La Warr Parade, c. 1900. One of the principal amusements at the seaside resort was the band concert and most bandstands were very ornate in style. Demand for seaside entertainment led Viscount Cantelupe to engage the White Viennese Band of Herr Stanislaus Wurm in 1894 to give concerts here. Later in the century this bandstand was removed to Egerton Park.

135. Bexhill Fire Brigade leaving their old premises in Amherst Road, a site which was in use from 1896-1971. As early as 1887 an attempt had been made to form a fire brigade at Bexhill and a volunteer force from the whole parish was established in 1888. The first fire engine, a 'Merryweather Steamer' was acquired in 1895 and remained in use for the next 26 years, c. 1912.

COLLINGTON WOOD

136. An early photograph showing the main footpath in Collington Wood. In 1919 this was purchased by the Corporation and became a popular recreation area.

137. The Maharajah of Cooch Behar opening the Memorial Fountain, 18 September 1913. This fountain stood for many years on the site of the De La Warr Pavilion; later it was removed to the Park and was subsequently dismantled.

138. An early beach scene, Bexhill-on-sea. Boating from the shore was a feature of the new resort during its Victorian heyday. The best known vessel operating at this time was the *Skylark* owned by Mr. James Gold who had been responsible for building many of the large seafront properties between Sea and Brassey Roads.

139. Beach huts at the 'new' resort, Bexhill-on-sea, during its Victorian heyday.

DE LA WARR PAVILION

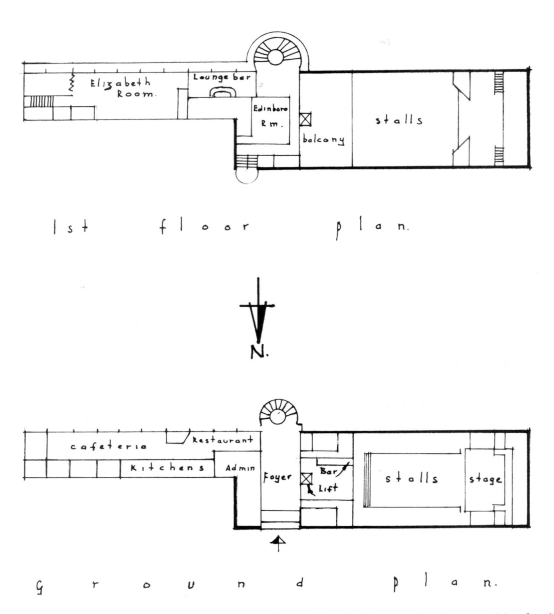

1st floor plan.

Elizabeth Room. | Lounge bar | Edinboro Rm. | balcony | stalls

N.

Ground plan.

cafeteria | Restaurant | Kitchens | Admin | Foyer | Bar | Lift | stalls | stage

140. The De La Warr Pavilion is situated on the seafront and was built as a result of a competition for the design, the successful architects being Erich Mendelsohn and Serge Chermayeff, two Germans who had recently come to this country. It was built at a cost of £80,000, and was completed in 1935. It was a building 'before its time', the concept of Central European designers of advanced architectural ideas for 'whom the British seaside, with its particular requirements for recreation and corrosive air must have been a completely unexplored field', to quote an official report on the building. Nevertheless, in spite of the original design not being wholly implemented, it has remained an outstanding example of continental influence in the 1930s. Photograph by courtesy of Rother District Council.

141. One of the few surviving pictures of the opening of the De La Warr Pavilion by the Duke and Duchess of York, afterwards King George VI and Queen Elizabeth, in December 1935. The then Mayor of Bexhill, Colonel O. Striedinger stands between the Duke and Duchess. Also in the group (left to right) are Earl De La Warr, Lady De La Warr, the Hon. Mrs. Geoffrey Bowlby (lady-in-waiting) and the Mayoress. On duty at the foot of the staircase is Mr. R. W. Hoad, for many years a member of the town's fire service, who kindly loaned the original photograph to the *Bexhill Observer.*

CENSUS FIGURES FOR BEXHILL-ON-SEA

Year	Population	Houses
1808	1091	180
1811	1627	268
1821	1907	311
1831	1931	372
1841	1916	411
1851	2141	429
1861	2084	447
1871	2158	456
1881	2333	548
1891	5206	1009
1901	12,213	2659
1911	15,330	—
1921	20,036	3510
1931	21,229	4911
1941	—	—
1951	25,668	—
1961	28,941	—
1971	32,898	13,755
1981	36,000 (estimated)	16,345 (estimated)

Notes.

1821   Population increased during the war, troops being stationed there in barracks.

1841   Emigration from all parishes in Bexhill District. 25 persons emigrated since 31 December 1840.

1921   Approximately 13.5% visitors.

CHRONOLOGY

772   King Offa of Mercia's charter granting land to found and endow St. Peter's Church.

1066   Bexhill devastated in Norman invasion; church lands later given to Rape of Hastings.

1148   Church lands restored to See of Chichester.

1558   St. Peter's church registers started.

1588   Cooden defences against Spanish Armada.

1561   Crown acquires Manor of Bexhill from See of Chichester.

1570   Manor of Bexhill granted to Thomas Sackville, 1st Earl of Dorset.

1597   Dr. Thomas Pye opens school in Chantry chapel.

1729   Severe damage caused by freak storm.

1735   Down Mill built.

1748   Dutch East Indiaman *Amsterdam* wrecked at Bulverhythe.

1755   Parish workhouse built.

1785   Bexhill Harriers established.

1795   Naval signalling station at Galley Hill.

1804   Arrival of King's German Legion at Bexhill Camp; first martello towers built; coal mine venture ends in failure.

1819   King George III's birthday celebrated by dinner for local veterans at *Bell* Hotel.

1825   Belle Hill Wesleyan chapel opened.

1828   Sidley Green battle between Preventive men and smugglers.

1830   Parish rectory built.

1832   Bexhill included in East Sussex Parliamentary division under Reform Act.

1834   Parish Poor Law duties transferred to new Battle Union and parish workhouse later closed.

1835   Princess (later Queen) Victoria attends meet of Harriers.

1837   'Turf' Wesleyan chapel at Little Common opened.

1840   Wesleyan mission founded at Sidley.

1842   St. Mark's church, Little Common, built.

1846   Opening of Lewes to Bulverhythe railway with station at Bexhill.

1853   St. Peter's Boys' school opened; Wesleyan mission started at Normans Bay.

1854   Hastings and St. Leonards Gas Company authorised to supply Bexhill.

1864   Prince of Wales (later King Ed.VII) attends meet of Harriers.

1878   Restoration of St Peter's Church.

1886   First main drainage scheme completed; Wrestwood waterworks constructed; *Devonshire* Hotel built; Mr. John Webb agrees with De La Warr estate to built West Parade and adjoining roads.

1887   Drill Hall opened for Artillery Volunteers; Ancaster House school site bought by Rev. F. R. Burrows; public gas supply started from Bexhill works; first piped water supply; *Bexhill Chronicle* started.

1888   Domestic piped water supplied for first time; streets of Bexhill lit by gas; first Volunteer Fire Brigade formed; Institute opened and Old Town Clock erected to commemorate Queen Victoria's golden jubilee of 1887; Egerton Park started.

1889   First election for East Sussex County Council, Bexhill having one member.

1890   *Sackville* Hotel opened.

1891   Wedding of Viscount Cantelupe and Hon. Muriel Brassey; restoration of Manor House started; St. Barnabas' church consecrated and parish formed; Institute of Charity allowed to open Roman Catholic Mission; Bexhill Golf Club's Galley Hill course opened; Harriers acquired by Viscount Cantelupe and new kennels built at Little Common.

1892   Reconstruction of Sackville railway arch; Salvation Army Corps started.

1893   Visit of Prince Henry of Battenberg to Manor House; St. Mary Magdalene's Roman Catholic church and St. Barnabas' School (now County Library) opened.

1895   Duchess of Teck's first visit to Manor House; Town Hall opened by Lord Mayor of London; *York* Hotel opened; Marine sea-front acquired by Urban Council; ornamental gates erected at De La Warr Parade; Viscount Cantelupe and Mr. R. Kersey apply for electricity undertaking licence (Later acquired by Urban Council).

1896   Viscount Cantelupe succeeds as 8th Earl De La Warr; opening of Kursaal by Duchess of Teck; opening of the Sackville Road Wesleyan Methodist church and East Parade cycle boulevard; *Bexhill-on-Sea Observer* started.

1897   Opening of Congregational church; opening of Buckhurst Road head post office; management of the Down taken over by Urban Council with De La Warr estate reserving manorial rights; Urban Council take over appointment of overseers from St. Peter's parish vestry.

1898   Beulah Baptist church and St. Barnabas' boys' school opened; first public telephone service with 33 subscribers; Grand Duke Michael of Russia attends local cycle races.

1899   Earl De La Warr goes to South Africa as war correspondent for the *Globe* newspaper.

1900   Consecration of St. Stephen's church, dedication of St. Andrew's church; *Metropole* and *Wilton Court* hotels opened; electricity undertaking started; Earl De La Warr's triumphant return from South African war; celebrations on birth of future 9th Earl De La Warr.

1901   St. George's Presbyterian church, Clinch Green cemetery and Down Artillery drill hall opened; Egerton Park and West Parade acquired by Urban Council from Mr. John Webb; first local omnibus service started.

1902   Bexhill granted charter of incorporation; borough divided into five wards and first municipal elections held; first motor races in England along East and De La Warr parades; Bexhill West to Crowhurst branch railway opened and Central station completed.

1903   First of 8th Earl De La Warr's two mayoralties; Cantelupe Road police station opened; first Whit Monday Horse Show; Manor House leased to Mr. August Neven Du Mont.

1904   Water and Gas Company Act of Parliament for Hazards Green works.

1905   Cooden home of Metropolitan Convalescent Institution and *Granville* Hotel opened; wireless experiments at No. 55 martello tower, Normans Bay.

1906   Mayoral chain presented by Baron Brassey; Lord Mayor of London opens Egerton Park extension; Hastings to Cooden tramway service opened.

1907   Lord Brassey elected first honorary freeman of borough and then mayor; Borough coat-of-arms granted; opening of St. Mary Magdalene R. C. church, Christ Church Primitive Methodist (now Springfield Road Methodist) church, Baptist mission at Sidley and first part of Down Elementary schools; Lecture Society founded; first public bowling green opened; Hastings gas works at Glyne Gap and Hazards Green waterworks completed.

1908   Hon. T. A. Brassey elected mayor; Town Hall extension opened and stone laid by Lord Buckhurst (later 9th Earl De La Warr); Prince Alexander of Teck (later Earl of Athlone) visits Church Lads Brigade camp.

1909   First part of All Saints' church, Sidley, dedicated; south aisle added to St. Barnabas' church.

1910   Death of King Edward VII and accession of King George V; first proclamation of monarch at Bexhill; Central Parade, town's first cinema and roller skating rink opened; West Parade collapse.

1911   Colonnade opened by 1st Earl Brassey; first aeroplane landing at Bexhill; further West Parade collapse.

1912   Opening of Cooden golf course and Cooden telephone exchange; Polegrove site bought by Corporation; P. & O. liner *Oceana* sunk off Bexhill and drifter *Gamester* beached after fire at sea.

1913   St. Mary Magdalene R. C. church consecrated; opening of the Good Shepherd and Malet Hall; opening of Haddon Hall Baptist church at Sidley; East and De La Warr parades acquired by Corporation and ornamental gates demolished.

1914   Outbreak of First World War; Bexhill Head Postmaster appointed independent of Hastings; Salvation Army Hall opened; start of Borough Museum.

1915   Death of 8th Earl De La Warr on active service; Bexhill Harriers dispersed; second Down drill hall opened.

1917   Bexhill Trust formed.

1918   The Armistice; Duke of Connaught inspects Canadian troops; first attempt to form public library.

1919   Peace Day and Ex-Servicemen's Day celebrations; Sir Leicester Harmsworth buys Manor House and estate; Collington Wood purchased by Corporation; first Maidstone and District Motor Services route through Bexhill.

1920   War memorials unveiled at Marina and Little Common; first municipal housing scheme.

1921   Old Town walnut tree removed.

1923   Official opening of Polegrove recreation ground; Rotary Club formed.

1924   St. Paul's Free church opened.

1925   Bexhill Corporation Act passed; Manor Court last held prior to Law of Property Act 1925 coming into force; Highwoods golf course opened.

1926	Borough acquired Bexhill Water and Gas Company; opening of Little Common Methodist church; opening of Secondary (later Grammar) schools; opening of Little Common recreation ground.
1927	Silver jubilee of incorporation of borough; formal opening of Grammar Schools by Duchess of Atholl.
1928	Regatta revived after 20-year lapse; London Road to Sidley compelted; Trams give way to trolley buses; Pankhurst's Mill removed to Leigh, Kent.
1929	Bexhill petty sessional division formed; first 'talkie' films shown at St. George's cinema, formerly the Bijou.
1930	Duke of York (afterwards King George VI) opened Little Folk's Home Annexe; All Saints' church consecrated and parish formed; St. Michael's church dedicated.
1931	Christian Science church, Devonshire Square, head post office and *Cooden Beach* hotel opened.
1932	First of 9th Earl De La Warr's three mayoralties.
1933	Bexhill Hospital opened by Princess Helena Victoria and Egerton Park Pavilion by Minister of Agriculture, Mr. Walter Elliot.
1934	St. Augustine's Church consecrated and parish formed; De La Warr Pavilion started.
1935	King George V and Queen Mary inspect De La Warr Pavilion site; Pavilion opened by Duke and Duchess of York (King George VI and Queen Elizabeth now the Queen Mother); Victoria to Hastings railway line electrified; visit of Lord Mayor of London; Christian Science church consecrated.
1936	Death of King George V and Accession of King Edward VIII; abdication of King Edward VIII and accession of King George VI. New Cooden Beach railway station opened.
1937	First television programme reception in Bexhill.
1938	Duke of Gloucester inspects Sports Centre site and visits Athletic Club camp in High Woods; Belle Hill chapel, oldest Nonconformist place of worship in town, closed.
1939	Second World War; Down senior schools completed; Bexhill reception area for London children.
1940	Large-scale evacuation of Bexhill; St. Martha's Roman Catholic church opened.
1942	Town centre damaged by 'tip-and-run' raids.
1943	Down senior schools brought into scholastic use.
1944	'Doodle-bug' raids over town; coast lined by anti-aircraft defences.
1945	V.E. and V.J. celebrations.
1946	Princess Marina, Duchess of Kent, and her children holiday at Bexhill.
1947	Borough electricity undertaking nationalised; Chamber of Commerce formed from Commercial Society.
1949	Borough gas undertaking nationalised.
1950	Borough re-divided to form six municipal wards.
1951	Princess (now Queen) Elizabeth drives through Old Town en route from Hastings to Lewes; Bexhill branch of East Sussex County Library opened; also Sidley primary school.

1952	Death of King George VI and accession of Queen Elizabeth II; Golden jubilee of incorporation of borough; Lord Lieutenant of Sussex (Duke of Norfolk) and Sussex mayors attend special Town Council meeting for conferment of three honorary freedoms.
1954	Roman Catholic church of Our Lady of the Rosary opened; Veteran Car Club rally on East Parade.
1955	New Rye parliamentary division formed to include Bexhill; Mr. B. Godman Irvine elected at general election.
1956	Duchess of Gloucester opens St. Peter and St. Paul junior school; re-organisation of local primary and infants schools.
1957	Lord Mayor of London opens printing trades convalescent home.
1959	St. Richard's Roman Catholic secondary school opened by Lord Longford (then Lord Pakenham).
1960	Silver jubilee of De La Warr Pavilion; *Sackville* Hotel closed.
1961	St. Mark's school closed; St. Mary Magdalene primary school moved to Nazareth House.
1962	Municipal water undertaking sold to Eastbourne Waterworks Company.
1963	Completed St. Augustine's church consecrated. Freighter *Aghios Georgios II* beached at Normans Bay after fire at sea.
1964	Closure of Bexhill West to Crowhurst branch railway line.
1965	Corporation purchase completed of Manor House and estate from Harmsworth trustees.
1966	Visit of Queen Elizabeth II and Duke of Edinburgh; first official visit of the borough by a reigning monarch.
1967	Closure of Bexhill gas works.
1969	Closure of Glyne Gap gas works.
1970	Revision of Bexhill county electoral districts.
1972	St. Peter's celebrates Charter (1200 years).
1974	Bexhill ceases to exist as a borough, one week short of 72 years; Bexhill Charter trustees formed and a town mayor appointed; Inner Wheel Club celebrates 50 years of charity work.
1975	Sea Defence scheme for West Bexhill coastline, public to meet expenses; Golden Jubilee of Bexhill Grammar School.
1976	Sea Defence Bill doubles in cost; 18th-century clipper ran aground at Bexhill.
1977	Princess Alexandra visits Bexhill; education in the town 'goes comprehensive.'
1978	Discovery of 15th-century Wealden house in 'Old Town'.
1979	9 inches snow fell; Bexhill was one of the worst hit areas in East Sussex.
1980	Bexhill's diminutive fishing fleet threatened by gale force winds.

SOURCES

Bartley, L. J., *The Story of Bexhill,* 1971
The Bexhill Chronicle, 1891-1930 (excluding 1905)
The Bexhill Observer, 1896 (excluding 1900), 1971-1980